The Opening of the California Trail

The story of the Stevens Party from the reminiscences of MOSES SCHALLENBERGER as set down for H. H. Bancroft about 1885, edited and expanded by Horace S. Foote in 1888, and now edited with Introduction, notes, maps, and illustrations by GEORGE R. STEWART

UNIVERSITY OF CALIFORNIA PRESS

THE OPENING OF THE CALIFORNIA TRAIL

Berkeley and Los Angeles, 1953

COPYRIGHT, 1953, BY THE REGENTS OF THE UNIVERSITY OF CALIFORNIA

University of California Press · Berkeley and Los Angeles
Cambridge University Press · London, England

Designed by Marion Jackson

Preface

THE NARRATIVE "OVERLAND IN 1844" IS THE MOST IMPORtant part of this volume, and most readers should turn to it first. In the Introduction I have discussed the general background of that narrative. In the Notes I have given additional information, sometimes at considerable length, upon special details. I trust that these are not without interest in themselves, but they will be better appreciated after the reader has some knowledge of the essential story.

I have been interested in the Stevens Party ever since 1932 when I began working on the Donner Party. The result of my work on the latter was *Ordeal by Hunger*. To write a similar book about the Stevens Party, however, was not possible, because many details are lacking, and because the details that are preserved are chiefly contained in a single source. I have therefore thought it best to reprint this source and to bring out its important historical significance by means of the Introduction and Notes rather than to write my own story, which could have been for the most part merely a paraphrase of "Overland in 1844."

I wish to thank the staff of the Bancroft Library and that

of the California State Library for generously offered assistance. I am also indebted to Professors Charles L. Camp and James D. Hart, and to Clyde Arbuckle, Francis P. Farquhar, Dorothy Huggins, and Irene D. Paden.

The Friends of the Bancroft Library have honored me by publishing the book in their series. I thank the Houghton Mifflin Company for permission to re-use two pictures already used in my *U. S. 40*. Finally, I thank Random House for allowing me to reproduce in scholarly form the material upon which I had already based *First Covered Wagons to California* in their Landmark Series of juveniles.

Contents

INTRODUCTION, 1

Overland in 1844, 46

NOTES, 93

BIBLIOGRAPHICAL NOTE, 113

ILLUSTRATIONS:

   The Murphy Party in the Sierras, 44-45
   Moses Schallenberger, 85
   Elisha Stephens, 85
   Present-Day Views along the Trail, following 86

MAPS:

   Route of the Stephens Party
      Council Bluffs to Humboldt Sink, 17
      Humboldt Sink to Sutter's Fort, 25

Introduction

THE GROUP OF COVERED-WAGON EMIGRANTS HERE CALLED the Stevens Party has been variously known. In it, besides Stevens, were individuals named Murphy, Townsend, Greenwood, and Hitchcock, and these names and different combinations of them have been used to denote the company as a whole. In addition, the name Stevens has frequently been spelled Stephens. Fortunately, the qualification "of 1844" has generally been added, and so no real confusion has resulted.

By whatever name, the historical importance of this party rests in its opening of the first wagon-road to California, and its discovery and surmounting of Donner Pass. Although historians have vaguely recognized this importance, they have generally given the Stevens Party less attention than its significance warrants, probably because the chief document relative to it has been comparatively unknown and not readily available.

This document also supplies the story of Moses Schallenberger, one of the great human-interest stories of the early West. Not only does it thus present a vivid tale of the adventures of a seventeen-year-old boy while crossing the plains, but it also enshrines his own narrative of his unique winter-long vigil at Donner Lake, in a snow-buried cabin, living upon foxes.

The purpose of this volume is to publish Schallenberger's narrative, and also, by means of an introduction and copious notes, to make clear the history of the Stevens Party, and its significance.

The Introduction will consider (1) The Text, (2) The Author, (3) The Personnel, (4) The Route, (5) The Chronology, and (6) The Leadership.

I

The Text

The document here called "Overland in 1844" has a highly curious history, and this must be understood before we can appraise its historical value.

When Hubert Howe Bancroft, with the help of a numerous staff, was collecting material for his history of California, he approached many pioneers for their reminiscences. Among these was Moses Schallenberger. Apparently the first request was that Schallenberger would check an already compiled list of the members of the Stevens Party. Bancroft states (*History of California,* IV, 446, n. 9): "My list has been revised by Schallenberger."

In preparing memoirs, however, either Schallenberger was dilatory or Bancroft was late in approaching him. Note 13 of the same chapter, as continued (p. 454), begins: "Moses Schallenberger's *Overland in 1844* is a MS. received since my account on p. 445-8 was stereotyped." A five-hundred-word summary follows.

In his "Pioneer Register and Index" Bancroft mentions under his notice of Schallenberger (*op. cit.,* V, 713): "His remarkable adventures . . . as related in his MS., *Overland in '44* [the change in title is Bancroft's]." The notice adds: "his daughter Maggie in '84-5 was a teacher, who from

Introduction 3

her father's notes wrote the MS. narrative of the overland trip."

What happened to this manuscript is uncertain. It is not now in the Bancroft Library. It is not listed in the "Valencia Street Catalogue," compiled before the Bancroft collection came into the possession of the University of California.

The tradition as preserved among the librarians of the Bancroft Library, for which I am indebted to Mrs. Edna Parratt, formerly a member of its staff, is that the manuscript was sent back to Schallenberger for additions or revisions, and was destroyed by fire. According to a letter from Mr. Clyde Arbuckle of San Jose, Mrs. Maude Weston, granddaughter of Dr. John Townsend and therefore grandniece of Schallenberger, believes that this fire occurred between 1894 and 1898.

In 1888, however, *Pen Pictures* had appeared. This volume, edited by H. S. Foote, is an elaborate example of the then popular compilation of local history and biography that is frequently called a "mug-book," since it contains numerous portraits of local magnates. Needless to say, these magnates paid—and plenty—for these portraits, and generally paid a smaller sum for a biography without portrait, although these payments may have been decently veiled as "subscriptions." *Pen Pictures* presents portraits of Martin Murphy, Jr., and James Murphy. There are good biographical notices for those two individuals, and a longer one for Bernard D. Murphy. There are also notices for others of the Murphys, and for Schallenberger, Dr. John Townsend, and Michael Sullivan—all of them members of the Stevens Party. Of even more importance, in an introductory section (pp. 38-53), under the subtitle "Story of the Murphy Party" appears the material here reprinted.

The situation is curious. The narrative, although most of it is credited to Schallenberger, is not printed along with his biography but appears under a title that does not use his name, and begins on a page opposite the portrait of Martin Murphy, Jr. We can only hope that Schallenberger received compensation in some form or other for having his reminiscences thus taken away from him and given to the Murphys.

The important question, however, is: "What relation, if any, does this account bear to the original manuscript that was prepared for Bancroft?" There is, I believe, no reasonable doubt but that the "Story of the Murphy Party" is chiefly based upon "Overland in 1844." In the first place, Schallenberger is several times mentioned as the source of the material, and it is unlikely that he would have written his reminiscences twice. Moreover, there are verbal resemblances between Bancroft's note and the text as it is now preserved.

From internal evidence we may effect a three-way division. About 15 per cent of the text is apparently based upon information supplied by John Murphy, Mrs. James Murphy, and perhaps other members of the family. Here can be included (1) the opening section, as far as the paragraph including the roster of the party, (2) the last two paragraphs, (3) a sentence near the middle in which John Murphy is cited as the authority. Other information, especially that about the horseback party and the Micheltorena campaign, may have been derived from the Murphys.

About 60 per cent is based upon the Schallenberger manuscript and is probably a rather close paraphrase of it, as is indicated by several such phrases as "gathering our facts from Mr. Schallenberger's narration" and "Mr. Schallenberger states."

About 25 per cent is directly quoted, and this part is introduced with the words "Mr. Schallenberger thus describes his experience."

My general conclusion is therefore that about 85 per cent of the present document is based upon the manuscript which Bancroft summarizes.

The next question is how accurately Foote, as editor, reproduced the original manuscript. As far as the section within quotation marks is concerned, we might begin with the assumption that he quoted verbatim. This could be,

Introduction 5

however, too optimistic. Dr. Johnson remarked that in composing a lapidary inscription a man was not under oath. The same can be said of the compiler of a mug-book. Yet actually there is, from internal evidence, nothing to show that Foote did not quote accurately, and there is one slight bit of evidence that he did. At one point three asterisks are inserted, apparently to show that something has been omitted. A more careless editor would merely have made the omission without this indication. We should remember also that Schallenberger was alive and in a position to protest overgreat liberties with his text.

In the larger section, based upon Foote's rewriting, we are doubtless much farther from the original. Here we may naturally expect insertions, omissions, and rewordings. We should scarcely believe, for instance, that the generally modest Schallenberger would suddenly refer to himself as one "whose conduct on the march had been conspicuous for coolness and discretion." In general, the section outside the quotation marks differs from that inside them by being more thickly peppered with polysyllabic words and by its often bombastic tone.

One small but important variation from the original can be demonstrated. Bancroft's note mentions the party as comprising "26 men," but our text reads "twenty-six persons." The former checks with the roster, and may be considered correct. I should suspect here an error arising from mere editorial fallibility.

Much more serious is the possibility of omissions. Bancroft gives no indication of how long the original manuscript was. Foote makes no statement that he is publishing all of it, and possibly he had to make cuts for considerations of space. Actually, I do not think that the manuscript was cut heavily. We must remember that it is a reminiscence, without notes, of a journey made forty years earlier. We should be amazed that Schallenberger remembered as much as he did, and should scarcely expect the original manuscript to have contained much more. Moreover, if there are any large omissions, the gaps have been concealed with considerable literary skill. Instead of going to the trouble to conceal omissions, Foote would have been much more likely merely to state that he was forced to sacrifice certain sections.

An editor, however, may choose to omit something for policy. I strongly suspect one serious omission of this sort. In *Pen Pictures* the narrative is really included as a eulogy of the Murphys. In the opening section they are extolled as pathfinders, not only above Frémont, but even above Columbus! After such a premise, Foote could hardly admit that from Fort Hall to Humboldt Sink the Stevens Party merely followed the wheel-tracks left by Joe Walker's wagons in 1843. (For a fuller discussion of this problem, see "The Route.")

There is also the possibility of editorial omissions from carelessness. A few of these may be suspected; for example, no date is given for the start of the journey, from Council Bluffs, although we should expect Schallenberger to have remembered the date and given it.

On the whole, however, we have every reason to be grateful to Foote. In spite of a few editorial sins, he has apparently preserved for us nearly all of an important historical document, and in an essentially accurate form. It seems to me, indeed, to be so accurate that I prefer to cite "Schallenberger" instead of "Foote" when referring to the 85 per cent based on Schallenberger's account. I have also thought it proper to use the original title. In any case, the title is an apt one, even to describe the parts of the narrative for which the Murphys supplied information. Thus assuming that we have here a fairly good paraphrase or reproduction of "Overland in 1844," we must next determine what the historical value of that work itself is likely to have been, and should therefore consider its author.

Introduction

2
The Author

Moses Schallenberger was born near Canton, Stark County, Ohio, on November 9, 1826. He was the youngest of the seven children of Jacob and Barbara (Miller) Schallenberger, who were respectively natives of Switzerland and Germany. When Moses was six years old, his parents died, and he was entrusted to his married sister. With her and her husband, Dr. John Townsend, he lived in Pennsylvania, then in Indiana, then again in Ohio. In 1842 the family moved to Buchanan County, Missouri. In 1844 the Townsends set out for California, taking with them young Schallenberger, then aged seventeen.

The story of this journey is the subject of "Overland in 1844" and need not be recounted here.

After arriving in California, Schallenberger worked first as a clerk in the store of Larkin and Green in Monterey. He resisted the lure of gold, but in July, 1848, working on shares with Larkin, he took five cartloads of goods to the mines, and sold them at high prices. He returned to Monterey in October, and remained there until 1850. In that year the Townsends both died on their farm near San Jose, leaving an infant son. Schallenberger moved to San Jose, took charge of the boy and the property, and remained a resident of that area for the rest of his life. He bought land, farmed it, and was moderately prosperous.

In 1854 he married Miss Fanny Everitt. He was a Mason, and a member of the Santa Clara County Pioneer Society. He died in 1909.

To Schallenberger and his wife were born five children. Two of these became teachers, one of whom, Maggie, attained a Ph.D. and held important educational posts in California.

This brief sketch is based chiefly upon the biography of

Schallenberger which was printed in *Pen Pictures*, and for which he presumably supplied the information. It is not presented primarily for biographical interest—and indeed, except for the journey of 1844-45, Schallenberger's life was uneventful. We should, however, know something about the man himself in order to judge the authenticity of his work.

First of all, we should note, he appears even from this brief sketch to be the solid citizen, a man whose word is likely to be good. Moreover, the intellectual achievements of his children are not without point. Like a poet, a Ph.D. may be said to be born and not made. When Maggie as a young woman and already a teacher wrote down her father's reminiscences from his dictation, we can feel a certain likelihood that as an incipient Ph.D. she was insisting upon some degree of scholarly accuracy, and that he felt, under the eye of a blue-stocking daughter, a strong sense of responsibility.

Although Schallenberger had only a frontier schooling, he seems to have been a man of high intelligence. Some of his letters are preserved in the Bancroft Library. Although he could not spell accurately, his diction and general command of language are excellent. Such words as "laconically" and "patriarch" would not, I think, be beyond him, although I admit my doubts about "equicide."

As regards the actual language, however, a question of authorship is raised by Bancroft's statement, already quoted, that Maggie wrote the manuscript from her father's notes. Mr. Clyde Arbuckle, a close friend of Maggie's until her death in 1951, writes me that Schallenberger "just dictated the facts to his daughter Maggie, and she did the rest."

The question, however, is not of great importance. Whether she took his dictation or used his notes, the daughter would presumably have kept to the father's facts, and he could have looked the manuscript over after she had finished. Doubtless she improved the literary qualities to some extent. If so, we must consider this to our advantage, since we have no reason to think that she thus altered the sense.

Volume IV of Bancroft's history, for which "Overland in

Introduction

1844" arrived just too late, was published in 1886. Since it would have been in press for some time, we may take 1885 as the date for the preparation of the manuscript. In that year Schallenberger was fifty-nine years old, and was to live for twenty-four years more. We may therefore assume that he was in full possession of his faculties.

Another bit of external evidence is of possible importance in establishing the value of "Overland in 1844." In the *Call* article (See Bibliographical Note) it is stated: "During the entire trip accurate notes were made of the aspect of the country and other items of interest; names were given to the rivers, springs, etc. which they discovered on the route, and these names were written down in the journal kept by Dr. Townsend and Moses Schallenberger. . . . [Stevens] appointed these men to act as secretaries, with the intention of publishing a book, but the whole of the writings were unfortunately destroyed." If this statement can be taken literally, it is of importance. First, it shows that Schallenberger, even as a youth, was considered both responsible and literary, and could be entrusted with the keeping of a log. Second, Schallenberger, having once written down such data, would be the more likely to recall them later on.

I do not, however, stress the matter. Actually, our narrative is weak in such details as would go into a log; for example, names of places, distances, and dates. Moreover, Dr. Townsend, rather than young Moses, would probably have done most of the work of keeping such a log. Finally, we should remember, the beginning of a diary is easy but the continuation is hard. Such a fine log as is supposed in the *Call* article might well have been begun, but not continued very long.

As I see it, however, the reliability of our narrative is indicated not so much by external evidence as by internal evidence. The nature of the document itself is such as to inspire confidence. If the writer tells of himself, that is obviously because he remembered such events better than what had happened to other people. He cannot be called egotistical, for he writes with modesty, restraint, and good taste. He records incidents in which he appears ridiculous and foolish. The story is told in simple and unembroidered style. It consistently "makes sense." It coincides generally with the minor documents, and where it differs, it seems to have justification. It checks with geography. It presents a reasonable, although scanty, chronology which can be checked once on astronomical and once on meteorological grounds.

Of most importance, the details included in the narrative are such as would impress a boy of seventeen and be remembered forty years later. As a general rule, one can state that reminiscences are unreliable as regards dates and figures, names of people and places, relative order of events, and the other skeletal data of history. On the other hand, they are likely to be reliable about colorful incidents, especially those in which the teller himself was involved. Such incidents comprise the bulk of our narrative, making it, in fact, more outstanding as a human-interest document than as a historical one. We can therefore have more confidence in it than if it included a large number of unverifiable dates and figures.

All in all, therefore, even though we possess only an edited version, "Overland in 1844" seems worthy of credence.

3

The Personnel

Lists of the members of the Stevens Party are given in the *Call* article, in Bray's "Memoir" (see Bibliographical Note), and in Schallenberger's narrative. Bancroft states (IV, 446, n. 9): "The most complete list is that in the *S. F. Call*," but adds that it includes names of people who went to Oregon. He continues: "My list has been revised by Schallenberger . . ." Bancroft's own list, occurring in the same note that acknowledges Schallenberger's help, is presumably the list as so revised, after having been compiled originally from

Introduction 11

the *Call* article and Bray's "Memoir." In his supplementary note (IV, 454) referring to "Overland in 1844" Bancroft states: "The Cal. company is given as 11 wagons, 26 men, 8 women, and about a dozen children." As might be expected, since Schallenberger had a hand in both, only slight discrepancies exist between the Bancroft list and that preserved in *Pen Pictures*.

Additional information about individuals can be supplied from other records, particularly from Bancroft's "Pioneer Register."

We can, then, believe that we possess a list that is good enough for practical purposes and that may indeed be wholly accurate. In fact, I think that we can accept the figures of "26 men, 8 women" and that instead of "about a dozen children" we can specify "8 boys and 9 girls." This adds up to 51. One of the few uncertainties is whether Ellen Independence Miller and Elizabeth Yuba Murphy, both born on the journey, should be included in this total.

Not only can we determine the numbers, but we also can identify each individual. The "26 men" are: Edmund Bray, Vincent Calvin, Francis Deland, John Flomboy, Joseph E. Foster, Britain Greenwood, Caleb Greenwood, John Greenwood, Matthew Harbin, ——— Hitchcock, Ollivier Magnent, Dennis Martin, Patrick Martin, Patrick Martin, Jr., James Miller, Allen Montgomery, Bernard Murphy, Daniel Murphy, James Murphy, John Murphy, Martin Murphy, Martin Murphy, Jr., Moses Schallenberger, Elisha Stevens, John Sullivan, John Townsend. (The spelling of the French names and of Stevens and Britain must be considered doubtful; I have followed the "Pioneer Register.")

The "8 women" are: the wives of James Miller, James Murphy, Martin Murphy, Jr., Allen Montgomery, and John Townsend; a widow, Isabella Patterson; the two unmarried girls, Ellen Murphy and Mary Patterson. The last is doubtful. She is not given in any of the lists, but the "Pioneer Register" notes her marriage in 1845, in California. Presumably, therefore, she came with the Stevens Party and was of marriageable age. Possibly, however, Mary Sullivan should be substituted for her in the list of women.

The eight boys are: William J. Miller, Bernard D. Murphy, James Murphy, Martin Murphy III, Patrick W. Murphy, Isaac Patterson, Michael Sullivan, Robert Sullivan. "Barney" Murphy was three; his brother Patrick, five; Isaac Patterson and Michael Sullivan, thirteen. Young Miller was probably ten or twelve—big enough, at least, to accompany his father on the trip through the snow.

The nine girls are: the three young, unnamed daughters of James Miller, Elizabeth Yuba Murphy, Mary Murphy, Helen Patterson, Margaret Patterson, Tedra (?) Patterson, Mary Sullivan. As mentioned above, Mary Sullivan should perhaps be rated among the women. Mary Murphy was two; the Patterson girls ranged from twelve to six; the Millers were probably very young, and one of them may have been Ellen Independence Miller who was born during the journey. Elizabeth Yuba Murphy, born at the camp on the Yuba, is included. She would seem to have an excellent right; in the course of the journey she was not only born but also, quite possibly, conceived.

To gain a clearer idea of the party we should analyze it by age groups. The ages of many of the members are known, either exactly or approximately, and the ages of most of the others can be inferred.

Four men are to be rated, at least by the standards of the time, as old. These are: Martin Murphy, Patrick Martin, Hitchcock, and Caleb Greenwood. The last may have been eighty (see "The Leadership"). Murphy was fifty-nine. The ages of Martin and Hitchcock are not given. Schallenberger refers to them as "old," but the opinion of a seventeen-year-old in such matters is not of great weight. Both, however, had grown children in the party, and Hitchcock had a grandchild who must have been about sixteen.

Balancing these old men were Moses Schallenberger and John Murphy, both aged seventeen. Britain Greenwood was about the same age.

Introduction 13

The other twenty men were probably at the height of their physical power. Stevens was forty-one, or thereabouts. Townsend was probably about the same age. Martin Murphy, Jr., and Bray were thirty-seven. James Murphy was thirty-five; Miller, thirty. Most of the others were probably under thirty. John Sullivan was twenty, and John Greenwood also was very young. Montgomery was probably in his early twenties.

Among the women, Mrs. Martin Murphy, Jr., was thirty-six; Mrs. Patterson, thirty-four. Mrs. Townsend must have been in her middle thirties. The others seem to have been younger—Mrs. Montgomery in her early twenties. Ellen Murphy was probably about twenty; and since Mrs. Patterson was under thirty-five, Mary Patterson can hardly have been more than seventeen.

The men can also be classified interestingly in other ways. Three of them—Stevens, Greenwood, and Hitchcock—were experienced mountain men. (See "The Leadership.") To these, as being experienced in wilderness life, must be added Greenwood's two half-breed sons. Flomboy was also a half-breed. Magnent and Deland, as well as Flomboy, were French Canadians; they were presumably woodsmen, although Deland is once described as "Mrs. Townsend's servant." Most likely he was a hired man of the Townsends, but why he should have been attached to Mrs. Townsend is not clear.

The others, in general, while not precisely frontiersmen, were backwoods farmers, undoubtedly skillful enough with axes and rifles, self-reliant and hardy, well used to roughing it. Montgomery was by trade a gunsmith; Stevens, a blacksmith. These were useful kinds of craftsmen to have with an overland wagon-train.

The only professional man was Dr. Townsend, and even he had few pretensions to gentility. Like many backwoods doctors of the time, he eked out his practice by farming. He had owned a farm near St. Joseph for two years before starting on the journey. Obviously, a physician was a useful man to have along.

We gain a better idea of the party if we further classify it according to family groups and therefore necessarily according to wagons. Schallenberger states that the party had eleven wagons, and Sutter gives the same figure in his letter to Vallejo (see "The Chronology"). Clyman's hearsay statement (see Bancroft, IV, 446 n.) that there were thirteen wagons refers to the party as it was when it left Fort Hall, and so suggests that two wagons were abandoned somewhere along the way—a definite possibility. Schallenberger identifies the owners of eight wagons: Hitchcock, Patrick Martin, Miller, James Murphy, Martin Murphy, Jr., Stevens, Sullivan, and Townsend. (At least, Sullivan's oxen are mentioned, and so presumably he had a wagon.) Without definite evidence we can assign a wagon to Martin Murphy, Sr., and to Montgomery. Whose was the eleventh wagon must remain uncertain. In the narrative Foster appears as a man of some status, and he may have had a wagon. Quite possibly also one of the ten owners already mentioned had an extra wagon.

These ten wagons and their occupants, listed individually, are:

1. ——— Hitchcock. With him, his daughter Isabella Patterson and her children: Mary, Isaac, Tedra (?), and Margaret.
2. Patrick Martin. With him, his sons, Dennis and Patrick.
3. James Miller. With him, his wife, his young son William J., and his three small daughters. Mrs. Miller (Mary Murphy) was the daughter of Martin Murphy.
4. Allen Montgomery. With him, his wife.
5. James Murphy. With him, his wife and their daughter Mary. James Murphy was a son of Martin Murphy; his wife (Ann Martin) was a daughter of Patrick Martin.
6. Martin Murphy. With him, his children: Daniel, Bernard, Ellen, and John.
7. Martin Murphy, Jr. With him, his wife and their four boys: James, Martin III, Patrick W., and Bernard.
8. Elisha Stevens. Someone must have been with Stevens to help with the oxen, but there is no evidence as to who it was.

Introduction 15

9. John Sullivan. With him, his sister Mary and his young brothers, Michael and Robert.
10. John Townsend. With him, his wife, his brother-in-law Schallenberger, and Deland.

There remain, unaccounted for and unattached, nine men. Of these, Caleb Greenwood with his two sons formed one group. They would have had horses but would have had no need for a wagon. An old mountain-man with his two half-breed sons would travel light. If necessary, he could arrange for some of his goods to be carried in one of the wagons.

The final six are Bray, Calvin, Flomboy, Foster, Harbin, and Magnent. Bray was an Irish laborer, probably working his way. Foster—as stated above, he may have had a wagon—is perhaps to be linked to the Townsend-Montgomery group. The others were hired helpers, or merely young men with their own horses, accompanying the train.

In addition to the groups clustering about the individual wagons, some larger relationships can be pointed out. The family of Martin Murphy, including his children, son-in-law, daughter-in-law, and grandchildren, totaled twenty persons. To these may be added, as connected by marriage, Martin and his two sons.

Another group was composed of the Townsends and the Montgomerys, who had been friends and neighbors in Missouri. This was a much smaller group, and even if we add Foster, it totals only seven. These, however, were all adults.

Of particular interest in the Stevens Party is the large Irish and Catholic contingent. Twelve of the men are known to have been Irish—the Murphys, Martins, Miller, Sullivan, and Bray. As Catholics, the three French Canadians must be added for a total of fifteen, well more than half the men. Some of the others also, even though they cannot be identified, may have been Irish and Catholic. From an American point of view this group must be classed as "foreign." Nearly all its members had been born in Ireland or Canada. (See also note 1.)

The dominating numbers of the Martin-Murphy clan—and of the other Irish, who would have been likely to hold with them—might well have led to trouble, but apparently did not. The Murphys were intelligent and able, and they probably realized that they must work by coöperation.

Of the equipment we know little. The wagons were presumably ordinary farm wagons with canvas covers. We know at least that the covers were supported by bent strips of hickory. The wagons were ox-drawn, and the oxen must have been excellent beasts to have stood the hard journey as well as they did. There was, to begin with, a good-sized herd of loose cattle. There seems to have been no lack of riding horses. There is no mention of dogs, but doubtless there were some.

Stevens had some steel traps along. Townsend had "quite a library" of books, as well as "an invoice of valuable goods" to be traded in California. In the whole party, except perhaps for the Pattersons, there is little suggestion of poverty.

By and large, the equipment was apparently good, and the personnel may be called excellent. The party was not burdened with too many old men, women, and children. Most of the men were not only able-bodied and hardy but also intelligent and coöperative. They included among them a physician and two useful artisans. Not even counting the half-breeds, there were three men who were familiar with the West and two who had previously traveled over at least a part of the route.

4

The Route

The route of the Stevens Party may be divided into three sectors. (1) From Council Bluffs to Raft River they followed, except for one cutoff, an established route for wagons. (2) From Raft River to Humboldt Sink they followed the tracks of the three wagons piloted by Joseph R.

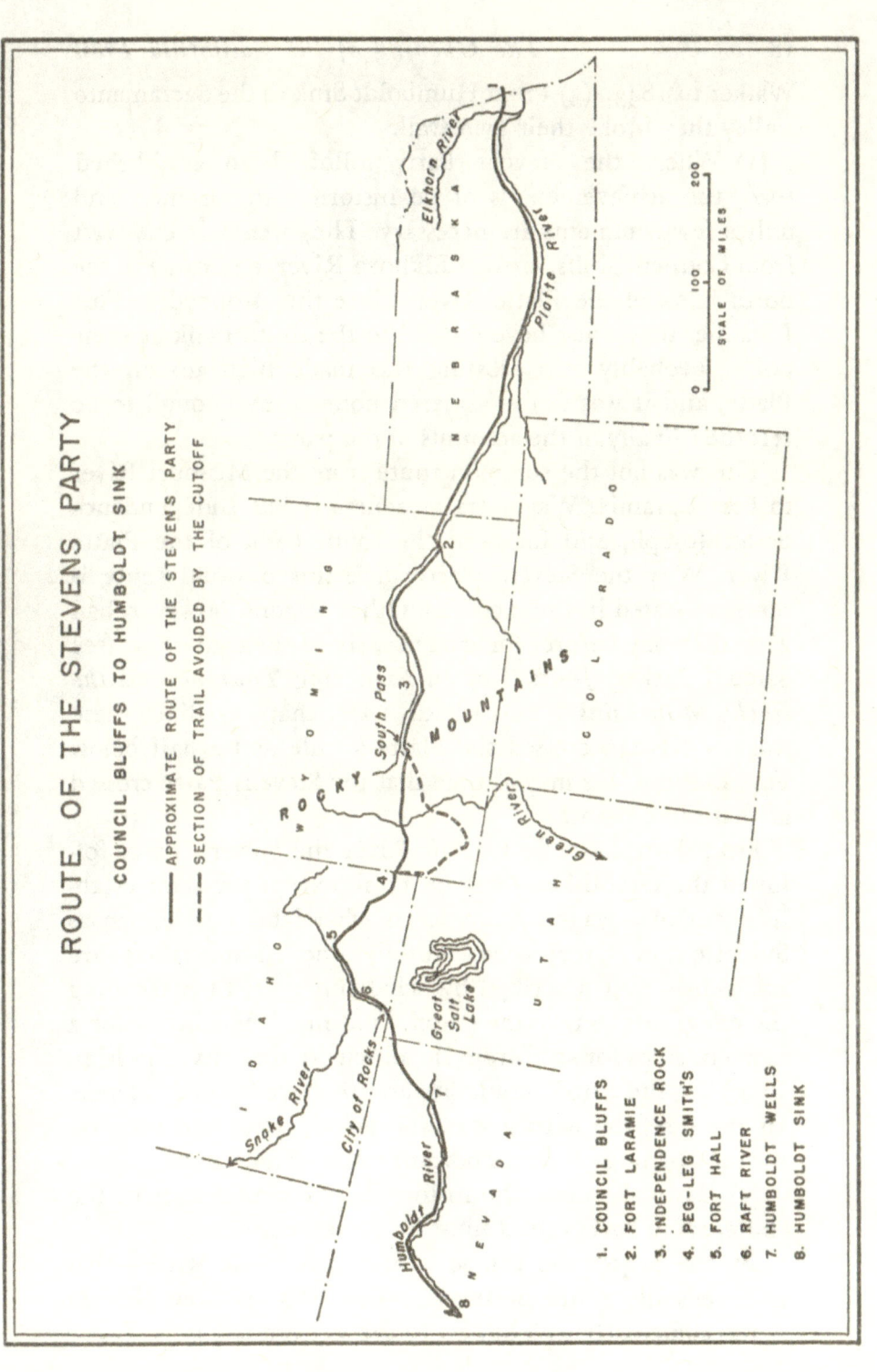

Walker in 1843. (3) From Humboldt Sink to the Sacramento Valley they broke their own trail.

(1) Where the Stevens Party followed an established road, the achievement is of no historical importance, and only a few comments are necessary. They went directly west from Council Bluffs, crossed Elkhorn River, and came to the north bank of the Platte River. Since they stopped at Fort Laramie, they must have crossed to the south bank at some point. Probably this crossing was made high up on the Platte, and it was not considered noteworthy enough to be recorded in any of the accounts of the party.

This was not the common route from the Missouri River to Fort Laramie. Wagon-trains generally left Independence or St. Joseph, and followed the south bank of the Platte River. Why the Stevens Party took this unusual route is nowhere stated in the memoirs. Other wagons, however, had gone that way before; for instance, six of them in 1835 (see Samuel Parker, *Journal of an Exploring Tour beyond the Rocky Mountains . . . ,* Ithaca, 1840, chap. 3). Since these wagons of 1835 crossed the Platte a mile and a half below Fort Laramie, we may assume that the Stevens Party crossed at that same point.

From Fort Laramie to Raft River the Stevens Party followed the established Oregon Trail, except for their establishment of a wagon route across what later was known as Sublette's or Greenwood's cutoff. The circumstances are sufficiently well described by Schallenberger. In persuading the emigrants to take the cutoff, "old man" Hitchcock for a moment steps forward from the obscurity that envelops him. By rights, the cutoff should apparently have borne his name. In any case, the narrative establishes the date and occasion for the opening of this important route of migration.

(2) To make clear the history of the second part of the route, some background must be presented.

By the 1840's the course of the Humboldt River—that indispensable route of travel across what is now Nevada —was sufficiently well known to the western trappers. There

Introduction

is no need to outline again the details of its discovery and exploration.

The first recorded attempt to reach California by wagon from the eastern United States occurred in 1841. This group of emigrants is usually known as the Bartleson-Bidwell Party. They left the Oregon Trail near Soda Springs, and followed Bear River until only ten miles from Great Salt Lake. From that point they set out in a general westward direction to reach the Humboldt River, or Mary's River, as it was known at that time. They were forced to abandon their wagons before reaching the Humboldt, apparently at the springs near the present Oasis, Nevada. The point of abandonment is established by T. H. Jefferson's *Map of the Emigrant Road* (reprinted by the California Historical Society, 1945), which notes "Chile's Cache" at this point. (Joseph D. Chiles was a member of the Bartleson-Bidwell Party.)

The exact point at which the wagons were left is not of great importance in the present connection, because they never reached the Humboldt and the route did not coincide with or even cross the main California Trail as later established and as traveled by the Stevens Party. The Bartleson-Bidwell Party traveled along the Humboldt on horseback, but in doing so they were merely doing what others had done before them and were not establishing a wagon road.

Far different was the achievement of the Walker Party, or Chiles-Walker Party, of 1843. Unfortunately, our records are here limited to very sketchy reminiscences, none earlier than 1860. There is enough evidence, however, to establish that the company had wagons, and that their route was the same as that of the later California Trail, from Raft River to Humboldt Sink. William Baldridge in a manuscript, "Days of '46," preserved in the Bancroft Library, states: "The outfit consisted of three waggons drawn by mule teams and a number of riding animals." The same man is the authority for the statement in the *History of Napa and Lake Counties* (San Francisco, 1881), p. 389: "From Fort Hall the party with teams, of which Mr. Baldridge was one, proceeded to the

Humboldt River, near the head of the north fork, and followed that stream to the sink." From an article signed "J. C. McP.," in the San Jose *Mercury* of April 21, 1864, we may quote: "Twenty-seven miles west of Fort Hall, our friends for this country [i.e., the Walker Party for California] turned to the south." Unsigned articles in the San Francisco *Bulletin* for July 20, 1860, and in the San Francisco *Alta California* for August 10, 1866, mention that the party arrived at the Humboldt Sink, but otherwise do not help to locate the route.

Nothing more seems to be available on the establishment of this important sector of western communications. Fortunately, something can be done by inference.

The unusually exact note that the party turned south from the Oregon Trail when twenty-seven miles west of Fort Hall can be taken to establish this turnoff to have been at Raft River. Actually the distance was probably nearer forty miles than twenty-seven, but exactitude cannot be expected. There is no other near-by place where the turnoff could have been made, and so we must assume that it was at Raft River. Since Schallenberger mentions "Raft River, which they followed for two days," we can assume that the Stevens Party kept to the route of the Walker Party here.

We have also the evidence already stated that the Walker Party "proceeded to the Humboldt River, near the head of the north fork." The question arises as to what stream is meant. The present North Fork flows into the main river between Halleck and Elko, rising in the mountains to the northward. It is incredible that a wagon-train turning south at Raft River could have arrived at the headwaters of this stream, and I assume, therefore, that some other one is meant. Probably Baldridge means what is now considered the main river. It might have been known as the North Fork in distinction from the present South Fork, with which it unites west of Elko. If we accept this conclusion, we can then believe that Walker brought his wagons across by Raft River, Goose Creek, and Thousand Springs Creek and

Introduction

struck the Humboldt River at or near the Wells. (See also note 17.)

From whatever point he reached the Humboldt, there seems to be no disagreement that he followed the stream clear to its sink, south of Lovelock.

From the sink Walker guided his wagons far to the south, by way of Walker Lake, intending to cross the mountains by Walker Pass. These wagons were taken across the present boundary of California, and so they were in one sense the first wagons to reach California. They were abandoned, however, south of Owens Lake and east of the Sierra Nevada, and so did not reach what was considered California in those days. Their route down the eastern side of the mountains was not followed later, and is of little historical significance.

From Raft River to Humboldt Sink, we must therefore conclude, Walker established a trail for wagons in 1843. There seems to be no doubt, moreover, that his trail was followed by the Stevens Party and that it developed into a part of the California Trail of later years.

As I have already stated, one of the most curious features of "Overland in 1844" is the lack of any reference to the Walker Party. This calls for more detailed analysis.

Even three wagons taken across country would leave a trail that after no more than one year could be followed easily. In a few places blown sand or floods might have obscured the tracks completely, but generally they would still be noticeable, and in addition there would be the plain evidence of broken bushes, rocks moved to one side of the way, and so forth. We simply cannot assume that an alert youngster like Schallenberger did not know that his party was following the trail of other wagons. It seems unlikely, moreover, that even in forty years, considering how much else he remembered, he would have forgotten this important detail. Certain questions then may be posed. Did he omit references to the Walker trail because he thought the fact unimportant? Or because he wished to aggrandize his own party? Or is the omission to be charged to the editor?

As I have already stated, I believe that the editor made the omission and that he had a definite motivation to that end. One sentence of the narrative may be quoted as possible evidence of this: "the remainder of the route lay for most of the distance through an unknown country." We should note here the words "for most of the distance." They indicate that the original narrative did not assert that all the trail beyond Raft River was entirely new. Although we cannot assume from them that Schallenberger gave proper credit to the Walker Party, they at least somewhat increase the probability that he did so. Moreover, for the section along the Humboldt, if Schallenberger nowhere states that they were following the trail, he also nowhere states that they were breaking one.

We must assume that the leaders of the Stevens Party asked questions at Fort Hall and learned of Walker's expedition and his plans. Did they learn of the outcome? The point is of importance, for on such knowledge or lack of it may have depended the decision at Humboldt Sink. We cannot, however, merely assume that, when the Stevens Party was at Fort Hall in August, any word had been brought of Walker's arrival in southern California about five months earlier. In 1844 communications were highly irregular between Fort Hall and California, especially southern California.

There is, actually, no good evidence that the party, at Fort Hall or anywhere else, received information about Walker's failure. John Henry Brown, in his *Reminiscences and Incidents of "The Early Days" of San Francisco* (1886), asserts that he rode east from the Sacramento Valley in April, 1844, and that he met the Stevens Party and told them how to get to California. But he makes no mention of Walker, and even if his unsupported and dubious story is to be believed, we cannot maintain that, having left an isolated camp north of Sutter's Fort in April, he would necessarily have heard of Walker's arrival in January, some hundreds of miles farther south.

The uncertainty of the Stevens Party at the sink, however,

Introduction

certainly indicates lack of confidence in the wheel-tracks as being worth following beyond that point.

Their hesitation may indeed show, not their ignorance of Walker's ultimate failure, but only that they did not know at what point they should leave Walker's route. Actually, if they had gone south at the sink and then turned up along Carson River, abandoning Walker's wheel-tracks at that point, they would have done as well for themselves, or better, than they did by turning west at the sink, and they might thus have established the Carson Pass route.

(3) From Humboldt Sink to the Sacramento Valley the Stevens Party broke trail for wagons, and may well have been the discoverers.

As regards the latter point, there is no good evidence that anyone had traveled that route before 1844. In later years two old mountain-men, separately, claimed to have done so. By that time, we must remember, that the "Truckee Route" had become famous on account of the railroad and that anyone who wished to play himself up as a famous "old-timer" would be likely to say he had traveled by it.

One who makes such a claim is John Henry Brown, in his reminiscences already mentioned. Brown offers the sort of testimony that drives a historian crazy. There is much in his account that is reasonable, circumstantial, and inspiring of confidence, and there are other things that are, if not impossible, quite close to being absurd. Bancroft doubted the story and noted (II, 732): "all this rests solely on his own statement," which was about as close as he could well go to calling Brown a liar to his face.

Also of interest, Brown says that a certain Greenwood was the one who originally told Brown's party how to reach California. But further discussion of this phase of the matter can be better postponed to our section "The Leadership."

A similar claim for the discovery of the Truckee Route is made by, or for, Joseph L. Meek in Frances Fuller Victor's *River of the West* (1870). Mrs. Victor states (p. 147): "they took their course along this stream, which they named

Trucker's [sic] River, and continued along it to its headwaters in the Sierras." Actually this claim is completely unfounded, for Meek was traveling with Walker's trappers of 1833, and they are known to have taken another route. The older suppositions that Walker actually crossed by Donner Pass have been refuted. (See Francis P. Farquhar, "Jedediah Smith and the First Crossing of the Sierra Nevada," *Sierra Club Bulletin*, Vol. XXVIII, No. 3, June, 1943.)

There is always the possibility, of course, that some trapper may have crossed by Donner Pass, and there is even the possibility that a document proving this may at some time come to light. At present, however, Brown seems to offer the only evidence.

Perhaps, however, the problem can better be restated. No less an authority on western exploration than the late Professor Herbert E. Bolton had a saying: "No one ever got there first!" By this he meant that the official discoverer always seems to induce a counterclaimant. Every Christopher Columbus has his Leif Ericson. The important question really is, not who first happened to be there, but who first solidly explored, brought back the word, established the route, and annexed the territory to the known world. By all these standards of judgment the men of the Stevens Party should have the credit for the discovery of the Truckee Route and of Donner Pass.

Their route became, with three variations, the western section of the original emigrant road to California. This is shown, mapped with care, by T. H. Jefferson (*op. cit.*), and may be found also in various modern books; for instance, in my own *Ordeal by Hunger* (1936).

The three variations of the later trail from that of 1844-1845 are of interest.

1. The Stevens Party, when they brought their wagons out in 1845, followed down the South Fork of Yuba River and then entered Bear Valley from the east. Probably in late

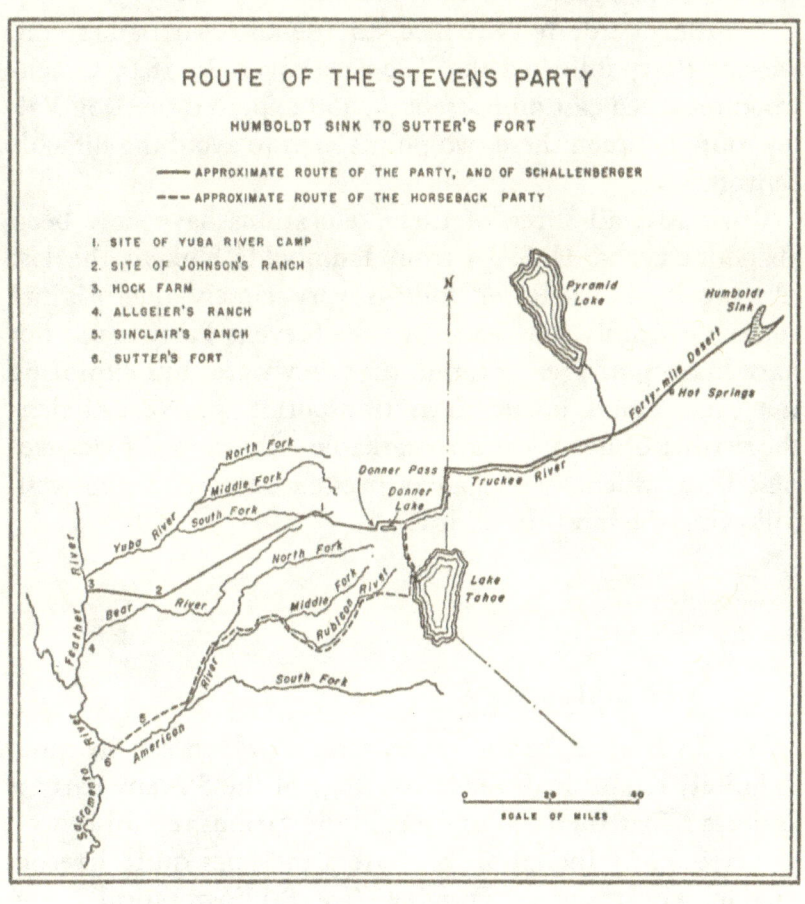

1845 and certainly by 1846 the road had been relocated to pass by way of Six-Mile Valley.

2. The Stevens Party brought their wagons over Donner Pass. Probably in late 1846, this crossing was abandoned for one via Cold Creek Canyon. (See notes 35 and 36.)

3. From Verdi to Truckee, to use modern names, the Stevens Party followed the Truckee River. In 1845 Greenwood returned east on horseback, and explored the Dog Valley route between these two points so as to avoid the difficult canyon.

Curiously, all three of these relocations have now been abandoned, and U. S. 40 from Humboldt Sink to the last crossing of Yuba River follows very closely the original route. Obviously, the leaders of the Stevens Party could not have known, or greatly cared, that they were thus exploring the exact route for modern transportation. Nevertheless, the verdict of history is a remarkable tribute to the doggedness with which those leaders pressed on toward the west, following the most direct line.

5

The Chronology

In contrast to the route, most of which can be quite definitely established, the chronology of the Stevens Party is confused. Statements as to time, in the various reminiscences, are frequently incredible and are sometimes quite irreconcilable. For instance, Quigley (see Bibliographical Note) dates the arrival at Humboldt Sink on November 10, and the *Post* article has the party already at Sutter's Fort on November 8, two days earlier! Only one event of the journey can be dated by contemporary documents, and even that one is not as accurately established as might be wished. Nevertheless, by the use of all possible means of confirmation, five dates may, I believe, be determined. Fortunately there is no

Introduction

dispute about the year, which was 1844, running across into 1845.

(1) May 18. This is the date of the start from Council Bluffs as given by Bray and in the *Call* and *Post* articles. An article in the Gold Hill *News*, May 5, 1875, gives May 20; a manuscript in the Murphy collection in the Bancroft Library, May 24. Since this is a date which is likely to be remembered, and since three authorities agree on one date and the others are not far off, I believe that we may safely accept May 18. The question arises whether this date of departure should be taken to mean Council Bluffs in particular, that is, the east bank of the river, or whether it should mean the departure from the camp on the west bank. I believe that it should be taken to mean the latter. The crossing of the river was a kind of confused two-day preliminary. The actual push-off must have been from the west bank.

(2) July 4. Bray states that July 4 was spent at Independence Rock. Although I do not consider Bray trustworthy for chronology, this is a date that anyone would be likely to remember, especially if it coincided with a halt at a place known by the name of Independence. Moreover, this date can be indirectly confirmed from Schallenberger, who went hunting from the camp at Independence Rock, was benighted, and had to travel in the dark. He states that "the moon was in the third quarter, but the night was cloudy." These are obviously details likely to be remembered by a man who was lost.

By "the third quarter" he means, presumably, according to common American usage, the phase more accurately described in most almanacs as "the last quarter." In 1844 such a phase began on July 7. Of course, Schallenberger was not an astronomer, and so might easily mention that phase as beginning a night or two before it was official. This would be all the more likely when he could not actually see the moon because of the clouds. In any case, the confirmation of Bray is close enough. From other details of Schallenberger's narrative I should make July 4 about the beginning of the week spent at Independence Rock.

(3) November 28. Just after moving into the cabin at Donner Creek, Schallenberger states: "It was now about the last of November or first of December." As it happens, just at this time the revolution against Micheltorena was occurring in California. In connection with the campaign Bancroft (IV, 468) mentions rain on November 28 and December 1. Apparently a considerable storm began about November 28, and this coincides with Schallenberger's statement: "On the evening of the day we finished our little house it began to snow, and that night it fell to a depth of three feet."

(4) December 10/13. A letter from J. A. Sutter to T. O. Larkin (see *The Larkin Papers*, Berkeley and Los Angeles, 1952, II, 318) is dated December 10, 1844, and reads: "I improve the present and first opportunity of informing you of a large party now arriving at this place from the U. States. Several have arrived from the Main Company—Which they left about One Hundred Miles distant from here." A letter from Sutter to M. G. Vallejo, included in the Vallejo collection (XII, 122*a-b*), is dated December 15, 1844, and, as translated from the Spanish, reads: "Day before yesterday, I sent you an urgent post to give information of the arrival of a strong company of emigrants from the United States with families." Unfortunately these statements are a little vague. The first letter apparently indicates that on or before December 10 the horseback party arrived at Sutter's Fort. Actually, I believe that these six had already been at Sinclair's ranch since approximately December 5. Although Sinclair's was only a few miles from Sutter's, it was on the opposite side of the American River, and undoubtedly the river was high. Possibly, therefore, no one at Sutter's knew about the Stevens Party until December 10. In any case the discrepancy is not great. The second letter is still vaguer, but it might be taken to refer to the arrival of the men from the Yuba River camp.

Introduction

(5) Schallenberger states that, when he and the rest of the rear guard arrived at the edge of the Sacramento Valley and camped on the banks of Bear River, "This was the first of March, just one year from the time they [i.e., the Townsend-Montgomery group] left Missouri." This is the only date that Schallenberger gives without qualification, and he gives it twice. The positiveness of his statement here, together with its coincidence with the original home-leaving, gives me confidence that this date can be trusted.

If we take these five dates as established, at least approximately, a fairly good itinerary can be compiled, by making use of different statements as to time, and by dead reckoning and comparison with the length of time taken by similar parties between the same points. (For more detailed arguments about the chronology, see Notes.)

PROBABLE ITINERARY

May 18. Left camp on the Missouri River opposite Council Bluffs.

June 20-24. At Fort Laramie. Bray states that the party made Fort Laramie in twenty-four days. This is an incredibly fast rate of travel for a wagon-train. Moreover, Schallenberger states that as far as the Sweetwater River "the emigrants had been taking things very easy." I have therefore changed Bray's "twenty-four" to "thirty-four."

July 4-11. At Independence Rock.

July 21-22. At Big Sandy Creek. This allows ten days for travel from Independence Rock. Schallenberger states: "They camped on Big Sandy twenty-four hours."

July 23. Arrived at Green River.

July 24. Schallenberger had his encounter with the Indians.

July 25. Left Green River.

August 10. Arrived at Fort Hall. This allows seventeen days of travel from Green River.

August 15. Left Fort Hall. Schallenberger states that they remained at Fort Hall "for several days."

August 17. Arrived at Raft River. In a note, Bancroft (IV, 446) states: "Clyman, *Diary*, MS., . . . says the Hitchcock [Stevens] party, with 13 wagons, left the Oregon company on or about Sept. 13." This impossible date results from a misreading of the source. Actually, Clyman makes the entry on September 13, and makes no statement as to the date of the separation of the parties. (See *James Clyman*, ed. Charles L. Camp, San Francisco, 1928, p. 98.)

October 1. Arrived at Humboldt Sink. (This is an important date to establish if possible, but the reminiscences are hopelessly at variance. Schallenberger gives "the first of October" but suggests the departure rather than the arrival. Bray puts the arrival about October 24. One of the Murphy documents in the Bancroft Library (CD-792:1) puts it late in October. Quigley gives it as November 10. By dead reckoning from our established date of July 4 for Independence Rock, I should make the arrival at the sink as about October 1. This coincides closely with Schallenberger's date, and he seems to be fairly accurate in the few dates that he gives.

October 8. Left Humboldt Sink.

October 9. Arrived at Truckee River, at present site of Wadsworth.

October 12. Left site of Wadsworth. Schallenberger states: "the party camped two days."

November 14. Arrived at the junction of Truckee River and Donner Creek. This is also an important date. In a letter to C. F. McGlashan when he was preparing his *History of the Donner Party* (see that work, chap. v), Schallenberger made a statement in which he declared that the party reached Donner Lake "about the middle of November." As I have already stated, I am inclined to believe any positive statement of Schallenberger's as to date. This date can be confirmed, approximately, by back-figuring from our already established November 28. (See also note 30.)

November 15. Arrived at Donner Lake. Horseback party set out.

November 16-19. In camp at Donner Lake. Schallenberger

Introduction 31

states: "Several days were spent in attempts to find a pass."

November 20-25. Moved the five wagons from the lower end of Donner Lake to the summit of the pass. This seems not too long a time to allow for the Herculean labor of surmounting the pass, as described by Schallenberger.

November 27-28. Schallenberger and the others built their cabin. I make the assumption that Schallenberger and the others stayed with the wagons that were being moved over the pass and helped with the work. They would then have needed at least part of a day to get back from the top of the pass to the wagons that had been left at the lower end of Donner Lake. Schallenberger, in his statement to McGlashan, says that they spent two days building the cabin. I assume these days to have been November 27 and 28, because Schallenberger also states that the snow began on the evening of the day when they had finished the house. (See above.)

November 28. The group with the wagons arrived on Yuba River, camped, and was snowed in. This allows a minimal time to break trail from the pass to Big Bend.

December 6. Seventeen men left this camp, for Sutter's Fort. Also, the horseback party arrived at Sinclair's. Schallenberger declares that they took "twenty-one days in getting to the valley." By "the valley" I assume that Sinclair's is meant. In setting the date I count from November 15.

December 10. The horseback party arrived at Sutter's Fort.

December 13. The seventeen men arrived at Sutter's Fort.

January 1, 1845. Sutter's "army" marched south from the fort. (See Bancroft, IV, 485.)

February 26. Martin arrived at the cabin. I figure backward four days from the following one.

March 1. Schallenberger and the others camped on Bear River.

6
The Leadership

Uncertainty as to the leadership is expressed by the five different names that have been used to identify the party: Stevens, Murphy, Townsend, Greenwood, and Hitchcock. From a consideration of the available evidence, my own conclusion is that the leadership, as with most parties, was largely coöperative, but that Stevens was not only the titular captain but also the real leader. In all the reminiscences except those representing the Murphys, the name is given as the Stevens Party.

In this connection one must note that family loyalty and even sycophancy has often determined what individual is given prominence. An amusing case occurs in a memoir of John Sullivan, who in 1844 was a twenty-year-old greenhorn, outstanding in no way. His eulogist, however, states blandly: "One Elisha Stevens was chosen as captain, but he was ably assisted by Mr. John Sullivan." (See "The Story of a Pioneer of Pioneers" in *The Christian Leader*, Dec. 22, 1906.) As we may here remark in passing, another point in favor of Schallenberger's narrative is that it does not attempt to make Dr. Townsend the leader.

We should, however, consider the various claims as to leadership, for by so doing we can, in any case, obtain further insight into the nature of the company.

Murphy. The first question to be asked is "Which Murphy?" The older Martin Murphy was a patriarchal figure, past the age of his physical prime. Martin Murphy, Jr., was vigorous and able. The younger brothers stand out less clearly. Generally speaking, when the term Murphy Party is used, no individual is specified. However, in the biography of Martin Murphy, Jr., in Bancroft's *Chronicles of the Builders* (III, 20), a strongly pro-Murphy account, the assertion is made that Martin Murphy was chosen captain, and

Introduction

that his eldest son was next in command. I take this as Murphy propaganda, and it actually seems inconsistent with what is said about Stevens in the same account (see below).

"Murphy Party," I conclude, has been used for two reasons. First, the Murphys were so numerous that by mere count of noses they tended to give their name to the whole party. Second, in later years the Murphys were not only numerous in California but also wealthy and influential. On the other hand, Stevens had no children and was living practically as a hermit, in obscurity. The biography of Martin Murphy, Jr., in *Chronicles of the Builders,* in spite of its pro-Murphy attitude, puts the matter fairly well (III, 19-20): "Although this company was piloted by Elisha Stevens, it is usually known as the Murphy party, from the number and prominence of the members of the family."

All this is not to belittle the Murphys. They seem to have been bold, and energetic, and were certainly talented at acquiring property. By standing together as a unit, as they must have tended to do, they could have exercised a veto power, and could probably have forced the whole party to any decision that they wished. But such mass power, though it may decide, cannot initiate. And for true leadership, therefore, we should look elsewhere.

Townsend. Dr. John Townsend was the only member of the party with professional status and of some education. He had a large number of books with him in his wagon, and undoubtedly some of these books dealt with the West. He was, I think, the only member of the company who could by even a stretch of the imagination be called a gentleman. He was also in the prime of life, energetic, and full of ideas. In fact, he was rather too full of ideas. In spite of being a doctor, his chief interest lay in get-rich-quick schemes. Certainly Dr. Townsend was an outstanding member of the party. He served as an officer in Sutter's "army," while the others rode in the ranks.

Yet again, though the reminiscences generally mention him in some connection or other, he is not credited with leadership. In "Overland in 1844" he appears occasionally, once as an officer of the watch, again as one of the three who rode ahead with Truckee to scout. We may suspect, of course, that the pro-Murphy editor of the narrative deleted passages about Townsend.

On the whole, however, we have little reason to think of Townsend as the leader. He had had no previous experience in the West. What scant information we have of him indicates that he was a talker, and a man of many ideas, some of them fantastic. He was less a man of action and of solid judgment. The circumstances of a wagon-train journey would soon enable the other emigrants to see through such a character. They undoubtedly listened to him with respect and appreciated his status as physician, but when it came to making a decision, they probably did not follow him.

Greenwood. The reminiscences give no prominence to Caleb Greenwood. The *Call* article merely lists him in an undistinguished place in the roster. The *Post* article does not mention him at all. In the Bray memoir the name Greenwood is written in, then scratched out; Hitchcock is substituted (see below, under "Hitchcock"). Besides listing Greenwood in the roster, Schallenberger mentions him three times. Two of these references refer to his useful but limited ability to communicate with the Indians, and imply strongly that Greenwood had never traveled along the Humboldt before. They give evidence also that Greenwood had no idea which route should be followed west of Humboldt Sink. Schallenberger's third statement about Greenwood confirms this: "Old Mr. Greenwood's contract as pilot had expired when they reached the Rocky Mountains." Just what point Schallenberger would indicate by "the Rocky Mountains" is uncertain. One would think that Greenwood at least knew the Oregon Trail as far as Fort Hall. Yet one incident suggests that Greenwood may only have known the country as far as South Pass. When the question arises of taking the cutoff from Big Sandy via Green River, the idea is Hitchcock's, not Greenwood's.

Introduction 35

But the star of Greenwood's reputation was destined to rise. In 1846 Edwin Bryant met him, and recorded some of his conversation in a famous passage of *What I Saw in California*. Greenwood then gave his age as eighty-three, although Bryant is careful to note that he records this figure "according to his own [Greenwood's] statement."

Gradually there has emerged what might be called a Greenwood legend. He has come to be hailed, though on slight evidence, as one of the greatest of the mountain men. Inevitably this saga assumes that he knew every foot of the West, and *therefore* he must have been the leader of the 1844 party.

His foremost advocate is Charles Kelly in *Old Greenwood*. Mr. Kelly, as a biographer, may be excused for being a great enthusiast for his hero. He is, moreover, almost unique among recent historians in having dug out and used the Schallenberger narrative. I cannot, however, altogether agree with him in the use that he has made of it. Having decided that Greenwood was actually the leader, Mr. Kelly seems to have worked upon the principle that whatever was done in the way of leadership was done by Greenwood. For instance, he credits Greenwood (p. 73) with finding the crevice through which the oxen were got up above the rock-wall of the pass, although Schallenberger—and Kelly seems to have no other source at this point—does not mention Greenwood at all in this connection. (See also Bibliographical Note.)

There is actually one bit of evidence which escaped Mr. Kelly but which, although dubious, may be cited in favor of Greenwood's knowing something about the trail to California. Here we arrive again at the tantalizing reminiscences of John Henry Brown (see also "The Route"). Brown states that in 1843 "a person . . . by the name of Greenwood" gave instructions to a party of trappers as to how to get from Fort Hall to California. Greenwood accompanied the party "as far as Hooters Damm," a place which no one can now identify, so well is it disguised by Brown's British ear and generally poor spelling. (Is Hooters a variant of Utah?)

Brown does not say that Greenwood himself had been to California. Even if we accept the story, Greenwood was certainly hazy in his knowledge, for he apparently gave Brown's party no information about the existence of Sutter's Fort. Again Brown seems merely to add to the confusion, not settling anything.

As for myself, I am doubtful of the Greenwood legend—both in general, and in particular as it concerns the Stevens Party. I doubt, for instance, that he was as old as he said he was. Even though he was briefly enlisted with the Astorian expedition (Dec. 3, 1810, to Jan. 6, 1811), this is no reason to assume that he necessarily was eighty-one years old in 1844. That expedition was only thirty-four years in the past, and Greenwood is much more likely to have been forty than fifty (and more likely thirty than forty), when he enrolled for such a strenuous undertaking.

As to his knowing every foot of the West, this rests largely upon his own statement to Bryant that he had been in California "twenty years ago." I am sorry to say that I myself regard Greenwood as a great deal of a talker and something of a bluffer. In 1845 he rode east to meet the wagon-trains and hire himself to more emigrants as a pilot. Probably in this year his name was fastened upon the cutoff, the existence of which he seems actually to have learned from Hitchcock in 1844. In the attempts to relieve the Donner Party in 1847, Greenwood apparently talked considerably, but he accomplished really nothing.

From "Overland in 1844" the conclusions about Greenwood must be mainly negative. He apparently did not know about the cutoff. He did not know the language of the Diggers, and apparently was unfamiliar with their country. He did not know how to reach California from Humboldt Sink.

This is not to say that Greenwood was not a useful man, and even an important one. He had made a contract, doubtless at so much a wagon, to act as guide over the first part of the journey. Actually, to follow the Oregon Trail in 1844 could scarcely have required a guide; but such services would

Introduction

have been useful for a knowledge of camping sites, road conditions, and so forth. Greenwood would have been useful also in any encounter with Indians, because he knew some of the languages, and undoubtedly knew sign language. Farther west, Greenwood had apparently no official position; he may merely have accompanied the party on his own initiative. But there is nothing to indicate that he was, even unofficially or at any time, the real leader.

We should remember something else also. To a group of Middle Western farmers and their wives, a squaw man like Greenwood, accompanied by two half-breed sons, would himself have appeared little better than an Injun and would have seemed a disreputable old rapscallion. They would have been ready to make use of his technical knowledge, but they would have had little respect for him as a person.

In this last connection we can note the interesting comments on Caleb and John Greenwood, as of 1845, by Mrs. Sarah E. Healy (see *Biographical Sketch of William B. Ide*, pp. 34-35): "They were mountain men, and dressed the same as Indians." In a note she adds: "I was more afraid of these two men than of the wild Indians." She was eighteen years old at the time.

Hitchcock. "Old man" Hitchcock is the enigmatic figure of the party. His first name is not recorded. Schallenberger gives him credit for the information about the Green River cutoff. Bray makes him important: "Mr. Hichcock [*sic*] was an old trapper, and mountaineer, was with the Subletts [*sic*] in their expeditions and gave us much information about the country to which we were bound." (In this passage "Caleb Greenwood" was first written, but has been scratched out and the other name substituted.) Concerning the route west of Humboldt Sink, Bray states: "by the advice of Mr. Hichcock we took the route he called the North Pass," by which is meant the route via the hot springs. Of particular interest, James Clyman twice identifies the party by mentioning Hitchcock (see Clyman, *op. cit.*, pp. 85, 98). Clyman, himself a mountain man, must have known Hitchcock, and for some reason considered him to be of sufficient importance to have his name put on the party.

This is as far, however, as we can go with Hitchcock. The evidence, when summed up, makes him a mountain man —unknown to fame except in 1844—who was useful for some geographical knowledge, who may have been to California (see above: "the country to which we were bound"), but who was neither officially nor informally a dominating figure.

Stevens. There is no doubt that Stevens was officially the captain. According to the *Post* article—and Schallenberger seems to confirm this—he was the captain of the combined Oregon and California parties until their separation. A brief systematic biography is therefore in order.

First of all we face the problem of the spelling, an unimportant but troublesome detail. We may question whether Stevens, or Stephens, knew how to spell his name. Or he may have subscribed to the principle of Sam Weller: "It depends upon the taste and fancy of the speller, my lord!" As officially recorded in the Kern County *Great Register* (1867) the name is Stephens. It is also so spelled by Baker, and in the *Call* article. A note included with some material kindly supplied me by the California State Library reads: "Name spelled incorrectly by Bancroft. Correct spelling is Stephens."

On the other hand, the writer of the *Post* article, who had had direct contact with Stevens, uses the *v* spelling. So does Bancroft. So does Schallenberger, who is never to be wholly disregarded. After considerable thought, I have decided for the spelling Stevens. The matter is of small importance, and is also essentially unanswerable. I think it better, at this stage, to follow the tradition of Bancroft and Schallenberger, rather than to search for some chimerical correctness. I must say, also, that I think the simple English *v* more suitable than the Greek *ph* for a man such as he was.

Stevens was born in South Carolina, most likely in the year 1804, certainly about that time. He was of French origin, doubtless of a Huguenot family. He was "raised" in

Introduction 39

Georgia and became a blacksmith. According to Baker's statement, "he early became imbued with a spirit of adventure and soon joined the wild and restless hunters and trappers of the great west." Baker also states that Stevens remained a trapper until 1844, and the *Call* article declares: "he has been a trapper twenty-eight years." A combination of these two statements would indicate that Stevens went west in 1816, at the age of twelve years. The figure in the *Call* article, however, may include an earlier period of trapping as well as the period in California. In any case, there is no reason to doubt that Stevens was a trapper for a considerable period, during the 'twenties and 'thirties.

According to Baker, Stevens "had ranged well over the Great Basin and Rocky Mountains" and had traveled "all over middle and western America." We must expect some exaggeration, and must remember that Schallenberger does not indicate Stevens's familiarity with the country across which the party traveled. Baker elsewhere records that Stevens had been in the northwest fur trade. This would seem to give a reasonable explanation. Stevens might have had wide experience on the upper Missouri, without knowing anything about the country along the line of the emigrant trail.

Some time before 1844 Stevens gave up trapping and settled in New Orleans, where he presumably returned to his trade of blacksmithing. Apparently, however, the lure of the West still held him, and in 1844 he showed up at Council Bluffs. He was no longer the mere trapper but had his own wagon. This made him a man of property and of responsibility, and so he was eligible for the captaincy.

The reasons for his election must be considered. He was certainly not chosen for physical charm. In fact, his portrait in profile shows an almost strikingly ugly man. To be sure, he was eighty years old at the time. The *Post* article describes him as slimly built, long-necked, with a misshapen head—long and narrow, unnaturally high-crowned. His nose was a tremendous eagle-beak.

He was, moreover, no politician. Although friendly and polite enough, he was taciturn, eccentric in his habits, and in later life at least, almost a hermit.

He had no family, and we do not even know who was traveling with him. He could, therefore, have had no faction to support him for election, though perhaps this very solitariness made him a neutral, and so a good compromise candidate.

His knowledge of the West must have been a strong point in his favor; but Hitchcock was also a wagon-owner and knew the West, perhaps better than Stevens did.

Still, Stevens was not lacking in positive qualities. The chief character-sketch of him is that presented by the *Post* article. This is in the nature of a eulogistic interview, and must be viewed with some suspicion. The language, it is also true, suggests the influence of phrenology, and so may possibly indicate what someone thought Stevens ought to be, rather than what he was actually. Still, all this admitted, the old man seems to have made a tremendous impression upon the interviewer. Stevens is credited in precise words with practically all the virtues: "cautious, polite, hopeful, courageous, prudent, plain, domestic, generous, attached to friends, firm, persevering and successful." The interviewer also adds, significantly: "he was born to command."

In this last statement we doubtless have the answer. Stevens was elected captain even though he was eccentric, taciturn, misshapen, and solitary. He was elected because his comrades recognized within him that strange power to command. It is a power, never quite to be explained, which some men possess and inevitably exercise.

That Stevens possessed this quality in a high degree we can argue from two bases. First, he was highly successful as captain. In contrast to other emigrant companies, the Stevens Party apparently did not suffer from quarrels. Schallenberger records only one small difficulty.

Second, Stevens impressed his contemporaries. Even if the *Post* article is to be discounted, the writer in the *Call* is con-

Introduction

firmatory. That article starts with the blunt statement, "Captain Elisha Stevens led the first company of emigrants across the Plains to California." We should note, I should think, the word "led." It implies more than a merely titular captaincy. The article also states that Stevens was "a man of sound sense and great experience," and its general tone implies his leadership. Bray, having mentioned Stevens's election as captain, adds later: "we had great confidence in our leader."

After his arrival in California, Stevens returned to the obscurity from which he had temporarily emerged. He worked briefly as a blacksmith at Monterey. He lived for a while in the mountains of Santa Clara County, and Stevens Creek preserves his name there. According to the *Post* article, he returned to the life of a trapper, "boating up and down the rivers and lakes."

In 1861 Stevens settled on a ranch which occupied part of the present site of Bakersfield. There, for twenty-three years, he continued to live an eccentric and hermit-like existence, busying himself largely with poultry and bees. He had not, however, lost the human touch. In 1863 the Bakers built a log house some miles south of the Stevens ranch. A few days later, as Thomas A. Baker (then a small boy) has recorded, "Captain Stevens came to the house with a crate containing six hens and a rooster. He said, 'Mrs. Baker, I know you would like to have a start in chickens, so I am going to present you with this outfit.' "

Old Stevens and young Baker became great friends, and Baker later wrote some reminiscences. Unfortunately, these were destroyed in a fire, and only some of his scattered memories are preserved.

In later life the old man apparently became possessed with the idea that he himself had been the real pathfinder of the west, and that Frémont had usurped his laurels. Stevens—old, obscure, and completely without recognition—had actually some reason for his resentment. Frémont had done plenty of exploring, and had arrived in California before

Stevens, but he had traveled on horseback and by a route so circuitous that it was of no practical importance. Stevens, however, had worked out a direct route and had brought wagons across.

Stevens died in 1884, the year following the publication of the *Post* article. By that time the railroad trains were crossing the Sierra Nevada by the route which he had pioneered.

History has not dealt generously with Stevens. Granted that others also deserve their credit, still they have been played up too much, in comparison with him, as heroes and leaders, and their names have even tended to supplant his in identifying the party. By all rights, also, his name should have been applied to the pass that was discovered under his leadership; but it is called Donner Pass. The map of California preserves his name only with little Stevens Creek, which rises in the mountains of Santa Clara County and, undistinguished, flows into San Francisco Bay.

THE MURPHY P.

According to E. T. Sawyer's *History of Santa C* *County* (1922), Andrew P. Hill won a gold meda Sacramento in 1878 with this picture, "which, cause of its faithfulness to incidents of the pio life of the state, was purchased and placed in historical room of the California Pioneers' Asse tion of San Francisco, but [was] destroyed by fir 1906." The present reproduction is from the Jose *Pioneer* of April 15, 1893. For the purpose black-and-white reproduction, some of the up part of the picture has been cut away. Hill, a lo trained artist, painted very realistically, and for details as the shapes of the rocks (cf. Picture

SIERRAS, 1844.

Overland in 1844

and the kind of wagons he is to be trusted. As for the route of the ascent, however, he had merely made the wagons follow the later Dutch Flat–Donner Lake Road. The introduction of the Indian Truckee into the scene at this point is pure romance.

Overland in 1844

MARTIN MURPHY, SR., WAS BORN IN COUNTY WEXFORD, Ireland, November 12, 1785. Here he grew to man's estate, an intelligent, industrious, and pious man, but dissatisfied with the meager amount of political liberty accorded to the Irish citizens of Great Britain, in Ireland. He married, at an early age, a Miss Mary Foley, whose family afterwards became prominent in America, two of them becoming archbishops and others achieving high places in commercial and manufacturing pursuits. Several children were born to Mr. and Mrs. Murphy in Ireland. As the family increased, so did Mr. Murphy's desire for larger freedom, and in 1820 he emigrated to Canada, taking all his children except his oldest son, Martin, and his daughter Margaret. He settled in the township of Frampton, near Quebec, where he purchased a tract of land and commenced to create a home. Two years afterwards his son Martin and his daughter Margaret joined them from Ireland. Martin, Jr., went to work at Quebec, where he met and married Miss Mary Bulger, July 18, 1831. The next year, the cholera having become epidemic at Quebec, young Martin purchased a tract of land near his father, and moved on to it with his family. Old Mr. Murphy was still not satisfied with his political surroundings and looked longingly across the border to the great republic, beneath the folds of whose starry flag perfect religious and political liberty was maintained. Finally, in 1840, he removed his family (except his sons Martin and James, with their families) across the then western wilds to the State of Missouri, and settled in Holt County, on what was then called the Platte Purchase. Martin Murphy, Jr., who, when he left Quebec, had settled in Frampton, bought land, hewed timbers, and erected a roof-tree for his young family, remained in Canada until 1842, when he sold his property, and, with his brother James, joined his father in Missouri.

The Murphys were essentially a family of pioneers; not from a nomadic disposition that rendered them uneasy unless in motion, but because they were seeking certain conditions and were determined not to rest until they found them. That no obstacle would stop them in their search for political liberty was demonstrated when they abandoned their native land to seek a home in America, and still further proved when they left the home built up in Canada, for the unknown wilds of Missouri. This second journey was full of inconvenience, and at that early day was an undertaking formidable enough to cause the bravest to hesitate. The course was as follows: Up the St. Lawrence River past Montreal and across Lake St. Louis to Kingston; thence across Lake Ontario and up the Niagara River to Lewiston, near the Falls; thence across the country to Buffalo; thence across Lake Erie to Cleveland; thence by canal south, across the State of Ohio, to the town of Portsmouth, on the Ohio River; thence down the Ohio to the Mississippi, touching at Cincinnati and Louisville; thence up the Mississippi to St. Louis, and thence up the Missouri to the Platte Purchase.

The location of the Murphy settlement was a few miles below the present site of the city of St. Joseph, but at that time there was nothing but a primitive mill used for grinding corn. The place occupied by our pioneers was called by them the "Irish Grove," in memory of their native land.

They had purchased several hundred acres, which they cultivated, and proceeded to lay the foundations of a home. Here was a rich soil, which responded with bounteous crops to the efforts of the husbandman, and here also was the perfect political liberty in pursuit of which the patriarch had traveled thousands of miles, encountering dangers by land and by sea. But there were two things lacking—health and educational and religious privileges. The virgin soil, covered with decayed vegetation, the deposit of centuries, was the lurking-place of deadly malaria, and, when turned up by the plow, the atmosphere was filled with germs of that dread disease, fever and ague, the scourge of the West in the days of its early settlement. There were no schools or churches, teachers or ministers of the gospel.

All of our settlers were attacked by the prevalent disease, and some of them died. Among these were his wife, and Eliza, Mary, and Nellie, daughters of his son Martin. Martin Murphy, the head of the family, was in anguish of mind at the condition of affairs. He was a devout Catholic and had reared his family in that faith. He saw his younger children and his grandchildren growing up in the wilderness with no religious instruction, and no holy priest to administer the consolation of the church to the sick or dying. The absence of these things was a heavy price to pay for the broad domain whose fertile soil would soon blosson into a valuable estate. While matters were in this condition the settlement was visited by Father Hookins, a Catholic missionary, who had penetrated the wilderness to administer the sacraments to those of his faith who located their homes on the outskirts of civilization.[1] He found the Murphys in much distress, mourning over loss of loved ones and full of anxiety as to the fate of others who were sick. He was a man of wide information and had traveled much. He had met brothers in the church who had described the glorious climate and fertile soil of California, a country which owed its settlement to the Mission Fathers, and where the cross was planted on every hill-side and in every valley, and which was under a government of which Catholicism was the established religion. All these things Father Hookins told the bereaved family in the days that he passed with them, trying to answer their eager inquiries with detailed information. As to the location of this wonderful land he could tell them that it was on the shore of the Pacific Ocean, and that it lay in a westerly direction from fever-stricken Missouri, but as to the distance, route, or character of the country or people intervening, he had no knowledge that would be useful to anyone attempting the journey. But in spite of this lack of all information as to how to reach this Arcadia, when Martin Murphy announced his intention to seek it, he found his entire family ready to follow him. We cannot sufficiently admire the indomitable mind that could make so great a determination with so little hesitation.

Men have made perilous expeditions upon compulsion or in quest of glory, but this proposition of the Murphy family to cross pathless plains and trackless deserts, and scale inaccessible mountains, with uncertainty as to food supplies and the certainty of meeting tribes of Indians, almost sure to be hostile, and to do this with half a dozen men and boys, with a larger number of helpless women and children, meets no parallel in history. The voyage of Columbus when America was discovered, contained no element of danger—only uncertainty. His path was defined; he would sail due west, taking sufficient provisions; if in a certain time he met no land he would return by the same easy route. It was a venture that required but a small portion of the courage, and involved none of the labor, entailed upon the Murphy party. Much has been said and written to the glory of Fremont, called the Pathfinder, who, two years later, crossed the continent. He had with him a large body of hardy and experienced frontiersmen, versed in all knowledge of woodcraft, and inured to exposure and hardships of all kinds. He had Kit Carson and his company of scouts, the most skillful ever known on the continent. He had abundant supplies, with a force sufficient to cope with any hostile band he might encounter. He had no women or helpless children to impede his movements, and he had the trail of the Murphy party to guide him.[2] In view of all the circumstances, the journey of these Missouri emigrants in its inception and consummation transcends everything of the kind of which we have any record.[3]

But little time was allowed to escape after the decision was made to seek the new El Dorado, and the first of March, 1844, found them with their belongings at Nisnabotna, a point on the Missouri River, in the northwest corner of Missouri, and about fifty miles south from Council Bluffs. Here they were joined by a party made up by Dr. Townsend, and they also found a large number of others, some forty wagons in all, but most of these were going to Oregon. Those bound for California were only eleven wagons, with the following-named persons composing the party: Martin Murphy, Sr.; Martin Murphy, Jr., wife and four children, James, Martin, Patrick W., Bernard D.; James Murphy and wife and daughter Mary; Bernard Murphy, John Murphy, Ellen Murphy, Daniel Murphy, James Miller and his wife, *nee* Mary Murphy, and family; Mr. Martin, father of Mrs. James Murphy; Dennis Martin, Patrick Martin, Dr. Townsend and wife, Allen Montgomery and wife, Captain Stevens, Mr. Hitchcock, Mrs. Patterson and family, Mat Harbin, Mr. Calvin, John Sullivan and sister, Robert Sullivan, Michael Sullivan, John Flomboy, Joseph Foster, Oliver Magnet (a Frenchman), Francis Delanet, old Mr. Greenwood, John Greenwood, Britton Greenwood, and M. Schallenberger.[4]

Notwithstanding the smallness of their numbers, they determined to go on, keeping with the Oregon party as far as their paths ran together; after that they would trust to their own resources to bring them safely through to the promised land. They proceeded north to Council Bluffs, where they organized the entire company for offense and defense. Mr. Stevens was chosen captain, and corporals of guard were selected from among the younger men. After laying by for a few days in order to make repairs and perfect their organization, the crossing of the Missouri River was commenced.

From Mr. Moses Schallenberger we have obtained many of the particulars of this famous expedition. The difficulties that met the party at this, the first stage of their journey, would have stopped many stout-hearted men. The wagons were safely crossed in a rude flat-boat, and it was intended to swim the cattle. The river was full and they refused to take the water, and when forced in would swim in a circle, trying to save themselves by climbing on each other's backs. They were finally permitted to return to the bank, but some were stuck in the sand, which had been tramped by them until it was as tenacious as quicksand. When the water receded, a few of the mired cattle were dug out with pick and spade, but others were fastened so securely and deep that it was impossible to rescue them, and they were abandoned. It was a question whether they would be able to cross their cattle at all. At last an expedient was hit upon. Two men got into a canoe with a line, which was tied round the horns of one of the gentlest of the oxen. The ox was urged into the water until he was compelled to swim, after which the men in the canoe could easily guide him. Other cattle were then forced into the stream, and following the lead of the first, they were all safely crossed to the other side.

They were now in the country of the Otoe Indians, a tribe which, though not considered hostile, had a very bad reputation for honesty. Of the people of the train only a few had crossed over when night came, and the young men volunteered to go over and stand guard. Those who were on the Otoe side were Martin Murphy and his family, and John Sullivan with his two brothers and his sister Mary, who afterwards married Mr. Sherbeck, of San Francisco.[5] John Murphy and Moses Schallenberger had been chosen corporals of the guard. They were mere boys in age, not over seventeen years, but were excellent marksmen, and had a reckless bravery born of frontier life. The wagons were formed into a corral by drawing them into a circle and placing the tongue of one wagon on the hind wheel of the one in front, thus making a very good sort of a fortification. The guard was placed outside of the corral and relieved every two hours, each relief being in charge of a corporal, whose duty it was to go from post to post and see that each sentinel was alert. While in places where the cattle might be lost or stolen, it was customary to graze them under charge of herdsmen until dark and then to bring them to the corral and chain them to the wagons. This precaution was taken on this first night across the river, on account of the bad reputation of the Otoes.

The time passed quietly until midnight, when the young corporals became disgusted with the monotony and resolved to play a joke on John Sullivan. The proposition was made by John Murphy, and indorsed by Schallenberger, though not without some misgivings as to what the result would be if Martin should detect them. But to be assured, they informed Mr. Murphy of the plot, who entered heartily into the spirit of the scheme. Accordingly, John unfastened Sullivan's cattle and drove them some distance into the woods, and he then gave the alarm. Sullivan, who it seems had all night been convinced in his own mind that the Indians were hovering about the camp, jumped up with his gun in his hand, and all joined in pursuit of the oxen. After a long chase, in which Sullivan was given a due amount of exercise, the cattle were again captured and secured to the wagon, Sullivan returning to his slumbers. He had barely got to sleep when the alarm was again given, and he again turned out, with some words not indicating much respect for the thieving Otoes. This time the boys had driven the cattle further than before, and the only way they could be followed was by the clinking of the yoke ring. During the chase, Sullivan climbed to the top of a log, and stood listening intently for this sound. John Murphy, who was lying concealed behind this log, when he saw Sullivan in this position, fired into the air with his gun, which was a shotgun heavily loaded. Sullivan leaped into the air, and, as soon as he could recover himself, ran at full speed to the wagons, crying out that he had been shot by an Indian. In the meantime the cattle were recovered and secured to the wagon, and Sullivan stood guard over them until daylight. He frequently afterwards referred to the narrow escape he had from the Indians in the Otoe country.

The next morning the captain, in commending the courage and skill of the young men in twice recapturing the cattle, expressed his surprise that Sullivan's oxen should have been taken each time and none of the others disturbed. The boys explained this by calling attention to the fact that Sullivan's cattle were white, and could, on that account, be seen better in the dark.[6] Two days after this event the entire train had been brought across the Missouri and was rolling toward the West. The "Horn," a stream encountered before reaching the Platte River, was crossed by sewing rawhides over one of the wagon boxes and thus constructing a rude ferryboat.[7] The wagons were unloaded and taken apart and put across the stream in this boat, which occupied much time and was tedious work. The horses and cattle were compelled to swim. This was the last stream where they were compelled to swim their stock; all the others they were able to ford. No striking incident occurred during their journey through the Otoe nation.

Arriving at the country of the Pawnees, they found a village deserted by all but women, children, and infirm old men. It seems that a short time previously the Sioux had made a raid on them and exterminated nearly all their able-bodied men. When the party received this intelligence they knew they would not be molested while in the Pawnee country. This gave them more confidence in grazing their cattle, but the vigilance of the guard was not relaxed at night. In fact, the Pawnees were not considered hostile; it was the Sioux nation from which they had most to fear, they being the most warlike, cruel, and treacherous Indians at that time known to the whites.

Before reaching Laramie, herds of buffaloes were encountered. The first were a few old bulls which, not being able to defend themselves from the attacks of the younger animals, had been driven from the herd. They were poor and scrawny, but as they were the first that the boys had seen they must necessarily have a hunt. After putting about twenty bullets into the body of one old patriarch, they succeeded in bringing him to the ground within fifty feet of the wagons, in the direction of which he had charged when first wounded. The meat was poor and did not pay for the ammunition expended in procuring it. However, before Fort Laramie was reached, the party were able to secure an abundance of meat from younger buffaloes, which is generally conceded to be superior to that from any other animal.

The party reached Fort Laramie with little fatigue and no loss. Here they found about four thousand Sioux encamped round the fort. They had their squaws and children with them, and for this reason were not considered dangerous, this tribe being loth to fight when accompanied by their families. While there was no immediate danger to be apprehended, there was great probability that, after leaving the fort, they would encounter a hunting or war party. These bands usually consisted of from one hundred to five hundred men, unencumbered by women or children, and never were known to waste an opportunity to take a scalp. The party remained at Laramie several days, having a good camp, with plenty of grass for their stock. They traded some of their horses for Indian ponies, thinking they were more hardy and accustomed to the work on the plains. They also bought moccasins to replace their boots and shoes, which were pretty well worn out by their long tramp. In resuming the march, still greater precautions were taken to prevent surprise by the Indians. The wagons were kept close together, so that they could be formed into a corral with no unnecessary delay. As the Indians in those days had no fire-arms it was thought they could be kept at such a distance that their arrows could not reach the pioneers. Fortunately, the party had no use for these precautions, for no Indians were encountered until the Snake nation was reached.

For so large a train, the party was unusually harmonious,

only one occasion of discord having arisen among them. This occurred while passing through the Sioux country. The orders were that no fires should be lighted after dark. This order was disregarded by an old gentleman named Derby, who kept his fire burning after hours.[8] Dr. Townsend, who had charge of the watch that night, remonstrated with the old man. Derby said that Captain Stevens was an old granny, and that he would not put out his fire for him or any other man. However, the fire was extinguished by Townsend, who returned to his duties. A few minutes only had elapsed until the fire was burning as brightly as before. Dr. Townsend went again to Derby and told him he must put the fire out. "No," answered Derby, "I will not, and I don't think it will be healthy for anyone else to try it." The Doctor, seeing that argument was useless, walked up to the fire and scattered it broadcast, saying to Derby at the same time, "It will not be well for you to light that fire again to-night." The Doctor was known to be very determined, although a man of few words, and Derby's fire was not again lighted. But the next morning he complained to the captain, who it seems had been a witness to the transaction of the night before. Captain Stevens sustained Dr. Townsend, and Derby, with an oath, declared that he would not travel with such a crowd, and he actually did camp about half a mile behind the train for a week afterwards; but he lighted no fires after dark. One day when the party had stopped for noon, some of the boys, returning from a buffalo hunt, reported that they had seen a band of Sioux. That night Derby camped with the train and remained with them afterwards, cheerfully submitting to all the rules.

John Murphy had been quite ill for some time, but was now recovered sufficiently to get around. He was anxious to go on a buffalo hunt and persuaded Schallenberger to accompany him. The boys were quite proud of their skill as hunters, and promised the camp a good supply of fresh meat on their return. They started early in the morning, well mounted and equipped for their expedition. They saw several bands of buffaloes, and followed them nearly all day, but in spite of all their strategy they were unable to get near enough to shoot with any certainty. Each herd had bulls stationed as sentinels on the higher grounds, who would give the alarm before our hunters could get within reach. Finally, the declining sun warned them that they must return. Reluctantly they turned their horses' heads toward camp, revolving in their minds the big promises they had made before setting out in the morning, and the small chance there was of their fulfillment. They had seen plenty of antelope, but to carry antelope into camp, when they had promised buffalo, would be considered a sort of disgrace.

On the return, however, the herds of antelope became more numerous, and some came so near to the hunters that Murphy declared he was afraid they would bite him, and, drawing up his rifle, killed one in its tracks. Schallenberger suggested that since the antelope was dead they had better save the meat. They dismounted and commenced the process of butchering. While thus engaged their horses strayed towards camp. They had only got about a hundred yards when Schallenberger, fearing they might go beyond recall, proposed to bring them back. Taking from his waist a handsome belt containing a fine brace of pistols, which Mr. Montgomery had made for him,[9] together with shot pouch and powder horn, he started in pursuit of the horses. He overtook them without trouble, and, noticing that a blanket that had been on Murphy's horse was gone, he looked for it on his way back to the antelope. Not finding it, he called to Murphy, who joined in the search. They soon found the blanket and started to return to their game and guns. Much to their surprise they could find neither. They hunted until dark without success, and then turned their unwilling course towards camp. They fully realized the ridiculousness of their position. Starting from camp with much boasting of the large amount of buffalo they were going to bring in, and returning, not only with no meat, but without arms or ammunition—the affair was altogether too humiliating. As they went along they concocted one story after another to account for their unfortunate condition, but each was rejected. The plan that seemed most likely was to say that they had been captured by Indians and robbed of their arms; but this story, after careful consideration, was voted to be too transparent, and they finally resolved to face the music and tell the truth. Their reception at camp can better be imagined than described.

The next day, with a party of six men, they went to a spot they had marked as not being more than three hundred yards from where they had left their guns, and, although they continued the search for several hours, could find nothing. There were thousands of acres covered with grass about four feet high, and all presenting exactly the same appearance; it would have been impossible to find their property except by accident.

Thus far on their journey the emigrants had been taking things very easy, and had not made the progress they intended, but they had no fears that they would not get through. Some of the party were getting short of provisions, but this gave them little trouble, as they were still in the buffalo country. They determined to stop before they got entirely out of the buffalo grounds and kill and dry enough meat to last them through; if their flour became exhausted, they could use their dried meat for bread with bacon for meat, and thus get along very well. Their route continued up the Platte and Sweetwater, the ascent being so gradual that it was hardly perceptible. They lived almost entirely on fresh meat, from three to five men being detailed as hunters each day. After going some distance up the Sweetwater, it was resolved to go into camp and remain long enough to accumulate sufficient meat for the remainder of the journey.

As the American bison, or buffalo, is now practically extinct, and their existence will soon be beyond the memory of even the oldest inhabitant, a description of this hunt may not be out of place in these pages. John Murphy, Allen Montgomery, Joseph Foster, and Moses Schallenberger started out at daylight, intending to hunt together, but they soon became separated, Murphy and Foster following one herd of cows and Montgomery and Schallenberger another.

We will follow the latter party, gathering our facts from Mr. Schallenberger's narration. They kept after the herd all day without being able to get within rifle range, owing to the fact that a picket guard of bulls was always kept on the highest points, who gave the alarm on the approach of the hunters. Finally they reached a large mound of rocks, under shelter of which they thought they might reach a ravine which would furnish cover within range of the game. They reached the top of the mound, and, looking over, discovered an old bull on the other side, fast asleep. To keep out of sight of the herd they would be compelled to pass in front of his nose. They crawled along cautiously, near enough to touch him with their guns, and they began to hope for success in their undertaking; but as soon as they came in front of his nose, he seemed to wind them, and, starting up with a snort, he rushed off toward the cows at full speed. Aggravated by their failure, Montgomery sent a bullet after the bull, which tumbled him on the plain. The report of the rifle startled the herd and caused them to move on.

The hunters followed them until nearly dark, when they stopped at a small tributary of the Sweetwater to drink. Here the men, by crawling on their stomachs and taking advantage of a few greasewood bushes that were growing here and there over the plain, succeeded in approaching within about two hundred yards of the game. It was now nearly nightfall, and although the distance was too great for accurate shooting, it was their last chance, and they resolved to make the venture. Selecting a good-looking cow, they both aimed at her heart. At the word "fire" both rifles were discharged simultaneously. The bullets struck the quarry just above the kidneys, and her hind parts dropped to the ground. The hunters concealed themselves behind the brush and reloaded their rifles. In the meantime the entire herd gathered round the wounded cow, sniffing the blood and pawing and bellowing.

While thus engaged, Montgomery and Schallenberger emerged from their concealment, and, advancing to about seventy-five yards, shot down seven of the best of them; but as they advanced nearer, the herd took fright and galloped off, all but one bull, which remained near the broken-backed cow, and showed fight. Two bullets were fired into him, and he walked off about forty yards and laid down and died. On examining the cow first shot, they found the two bullet-holes not two inches apart, but neither one was within three feet of the point aimed at.

It was now quite dark, and they could not return to camp. Accordingly, they made their bed between the carcasses of the two cows, and, butchering the others, carried the meat to this place to protect it from the wolves. These animals gathered in large numbers and made night hideous until, towards morning, they were driven off by a huge bear, who had come for his breakfast. As soon as it became light enough to shoot, Montgomery and Schallenberger attempted to kill the bear, but he went away so rapidly that they could not follow him. After returning from pursuit of the bear, they finished butchering their game, which process consisted of cutting out the choice pieces and leaving the rest to the wolves. Packing the meat on their horses, they started for camp about three o'clock in the afternoon. They traveled until after dark, but could find no camp. The moon was in the third quarter, but the night was cloudy, and they became bewildered. They traveled all night, walking and leading their horses. At daybreak they crossed the trail of the wagons about a quarter of a mile from camp. They arrived at the wagons just as the guard was taken off. They were nearly worn out with fatigue, but Schallenberger says he felt a great deal more cheerful than when he and Murphy came into camp with neither meat nor arms. The other hunting parties had been equally successfully [*sic*], and a week was spent in this camp killing and curing meat, after which they resumed their journey up the Sweetwater. In this camp was born to Mr. and Mrs. James Miller a daughter, who was named Ellen Independence, from Independence Rock, which was near the place.

They continued sending out hunting parties until they reached the summit of the Rocky Mountains, when the buffalo disappeared. There was still plenty of deer and antelope, which rendered it unnecessary to draw on their supply of dried meat. On reaching the summit they saw that the water ran towards California, and their hearts were rejoiced as though already in sight of the promised land. They had no idea of how much farther they had to go. They had already come hundreds of miles and naturally supposed that their journey was nearing its end. Neither did they realize that they were still to encounter obstacles almost insurmountable and undergo hardships compared to which their journey thus far had been a pleasure excursion.

The emigrants now moved towards Green River, by way of Little and Big Sandy. They camped on Big Sandy twenty-four hours, and there old man Hitchcock was appointed pilot for one day, he saying that, from information he had, he could take them to Green River by a cut-off that would save a hundred miles' travel. By this route he thought the distance from Big Sandy to Green River was about twenty-five miles.[10] Not knowing the character of the country, and thinking the distance was short, the emigrants did not prepare a supply of water to take with them, as they might have done and saved themselves much suffering.

Starting at daylight they traveled until dark, most of the distance being across a rough, broken country, but found no Green River or water of any kind. At last they were compelled to halt in the midst of a desolate country, tired and nearly famished for water. The poor cattle suffered terribly, and notwithstanding their precautions in herding them, about forty head of cows and young cattle broke away in the night. The next morning they pushed forward as soon as it was light enough to see, and at eleven o'clock reached Green River.

This was their first real hardship on the march, and, coming unexpectedly, it found them unprepared, and their sufferings were much greater than they otherwise would have been. The next morning after their arrival at Green River, they detailed six men to hunt for the cattle that had broken loose on the march from Big Sandy. This detail consisted of Daniel Murphy, William Higgins, Mr. Bean, Perry Derby, Mat Harbin and Moses Schallenberger.[11] After starting on the hunt, a difference of opinion arose as to the route the cattle had taken. Murphy, Schallenberger, and Bean thought they had taken the back track to the Big Sandy; the others thought they had made for the nearest water, which was at Green River, some twelve miles below the point reached by the emigrants.

Not being able to agree, they divided the party, Murphy, Bean, and Schallenberger going back to the Sandy. About half way across, while this party were riding along in Indian file, Murphy, who was in advance, suddenly ducked his head, threw his body over to the side of his horse, and, wheeling round, signaled to the others to do the same. They obeyed, and, putting their horses to full speed, followed Murphy to a small cañon, which they ascended for a quarter of a mile. During this time not a word had been spoken, but now, coming to a halt, they inquired what was the matter. Murphy laconically replied, "Indians." The party dismounted and tied their horses, and, getting down on their stomachs, crawled to a point where they could overlook the plain. Here they discovered a war party of about a hundred Sioux, who were so near that their conversation could be distinctly heard. They passed within twenty yards of the spot where our emigrants were concealed, without discovering them, and the little party drew a long breath of relief when the last feathered top-knot disappeared down the horizon. It was a close call, for had their presence been known, the little band of whites would never have seen the golden plains of California.

Again mounting their horses, they proceeded to the Big Sandy, where they found all the missing cattle. Gathering them up, they passed the night in their old camp, and the next morning set out on their return to Green River. They had proceeded only half a mile when they discovered two Indians on horseback on the top of a hill about a mile distant. In a couple of minutes, two more made their appearance in another direction, and within ten minutes they were surrounded by a couple of hundred Indians, all whooping and charging in a manner to strike terror to the bravest heart. There seemed no escape, but the little party resolved to sell their lives as dearly as possible. In the short time they had for consultation, it was determined that when they approached within range each man should select his Indian, shoot him, and then charge, trusting to Providence to get through to camp. They said good-by to each other and waited the onset.

About twenty of the Indians were in advance of their party, and when these had approached to a distance of two hundred yards, the emigrants signed to them to stop. This they did, and sent three men without arms to parley. These came on until they were only fifty yards distant, when they halted and held out their hands as a sign of friendship. Schallenberger says that at this sign their hair, which up to this time had been standing as erect as the quills on the back of a porcupine, began to resume its proper position, and their blood, which had been jumping through their veins like a race-horse, reduced its pace to a moderate gait. The Indians proved to be a party of friendly Snakes, who were in pursuit of the band of Sioux from which our party had had such a narrow escape the day before. They were very friendly, and some of them accompanied our friends to assist them in driving their cattle quite a distance on their way back to Green River, which they reached about nine o'clock at night.

The route of the emigrants now lay across a broken country to Bear River, where they found old "Peg-leg" Smith, as he was called.[12] He was one of the earliest trappers of the Rocky Mountains, and was living alone in the hills. He had a band of fat ponies, which he exchanged for some of the poor and tired horses of the train. Proceeding down Bear River, they arrived without adventure at Fort Hall, which was the point at which the Oregon party was to separate from those going to California.[13] Here they were compelled to purchase flour, for which they paid a dollar a pound. The Murphy-Townsend party had started with a supply of provisions sufficient for eight months, but others were not so well provided.[14] In fact, several had run out of flour and bacon some time previously, and the others had divided with them. As for meat, the party thought they had plenty; if their dried meat and bacon became exhausted, they could kill the young cattle they had brought along for that purpose. The parting with the Oregon party was a sad one. During the long journey across the plains, many strong friendships had been formed, and the separation was deeply regretted by all. Our emigrant train now consisted of eleven wagons and twenty-six persons,[15] all as determined to push on to California as on the day they left Council Bluffs. The country they had traversed was more or less known to trappers and hunters, and there had not been much danger of losing their way; neither were the obstacles very formidable. But the remainder of the route lay for most of the distance through an unknown country, through which they must find their way without map, chart, or guide, and, with diminished numbers, overcome obstacles the magnitude of which none of them had any conception.[16]

After remaining at Fort Hall for several days, the party resumed its march, crossing the country to Beaver Creek, or Raft River, which they followed for two days; thence westward over a broken country to Goose Creek; thence to the head-waters of Mary's River, or the Humboldt, as it has since been named.[17] Here they encountered the Digger Indians. The language of this tribe was unknown to old man Greenwood, who had hitherto acted as pilot and interpreter, but by use of signs and some few words of the Snake language, he managed to converse with them in a limited way.[18] The journey down the Humboldt was very monotonous. Each day's events were substantially a repetition of those of the day before.

There was plenty of good grass, and the party was not inconvenienced by the alkali water, which caused so much trouble to trains that afterwards came over this route. The Indians seemed to be the most indolent and degraded of any that the party had yet encountered. They were totally without energy. They seemed very friendly and every night hundreds of them visited the camp.[19] This they continued to do during the entire journey down the Humboldt, a distance of five hundred miles.[20] Although they showed no signs of hostility, the emigrants did not relax their vigilance, and guard duty was strictly performed. At the sink of the Humboldt, the alkali became troublesome, and it was with difficulty that pure water was procured either for the people or the cattle. However, no stock was lost, excepting one pony belonging to Martin Murphy, Sr., which was stolen. The party stopped at the sink for a week in order to rest the cattle and lay out their future course.

Mr. Schallenberger states that their oxen were in tolerably good condition; their feet were as sound and much harder, and except that they needed a little rest, they were really better prepared for work than when they left Missouri. The party seemed to have plenty of provisions, and the only doubtful question was the route they should pursue. A desert lay before them, and it was necessary that they should make no mistake in the choice of a route.[21] Old Mr. Greenwood's contract as pilot had expired when they reached the Rocky Mountains. Beyond that he did not pretend to know anything.[22] Many anxious consultations were held, some contending that they should follow a southerly course, and others held that they should go due west. Finally, an old Indian was found, called Truckee, with whom old man Green[wood] talked by means of signs and diagrams drawn on the ground.[23] From him it was learned that fifty or sixty miles to the west there was a river that flowed easterly from the mountains, and that along this stream there were large trees and good grass. Acting on this information, Dr. Townsend, Captain Stevens, and Joseph Foster, taking Truckee as a guide, started out to explore this route, and after three days returned, reporting that they had found the river just as the Indian had described it. Although there was still a doubt in the minds of some as to whether this was the proper route to take, none held back when the time came to start. In fact, there was no time for further discussion.

It was now the first of October,[24] and they could see that if a heavy fall of snow should overtake them while yet in the mountains, it would be almost impossible for them to get through. Thus far there had been no trouble with the Indians. All that they had met had been treated kindly, and the natives had rather assisted than impeded them in their journey. It had, however, required constant watching on the part of the older men to prevent the hot blood of the younger ones from boiling over now and then. This was particularly the case with John Greenwood, who, being a half-breed, had a mortal hatred for the Indians. On several occasions, when an ox would stray away, he would accuse the natives of having stolen it, and it would require the utmost exercise of authority to prevent him from precipitating hostilities. It seemed as if he was more anxious to kill an Indian than to reach California.[25]

On the morning that the start was made from the sink of the Humboldt, a general engagement became very imminent. Schallenberger, whose conduct on the march had been conspicuous for coolness and discretion, missed a halter from his horse, and on searching for it saw one end projecting from under the short feather blanket[26] worn by an Indian who was standing near. Schallenberger demanded the halter, but the Indian paid no attention; he then attempted to explain to him what he wanted, but the Indian pretended that he did not understand. He then took hold of the halter to remove it, when the Indian stepped back and drew his bow. Schallenberger ran to the wagon, took his rifle, and drew a bead on the redskin, and was about to pull the trigger when Martin Murphy rushed in and threw up the muzzle of the gun. The whole camp was in confusion in a moment, but the matter was explained, and the Indians [were] loaded with presents until they were pacified. If the Indian had been killed, there is no doubt that the entire party would have been massacred. It did not need the reprimand that Schallenberger received from his brother-in-law, Dr. Townsend, to convince him of his folly, and no one regretted his rashness more than he himself did.

The party left the sink of the Humboldt, having cooked two days' rations and filled all the available vessels with water. After traveling with scarcely a halt until twelve o'clock the next night, they reached a boiling spring at what is now Hot Spring Station, on the Central Pacific Railroad.[27] Here they halted two hours to permit the oxen to rest. Some of the party dipped water from the spring into tubs, and allowed it to cool for the use of the cattle. It was a sad experiment, for those oxen that drank it became very sick. Resuming the march, they traveled steadily until two o'clock the next day, when they reached the river, which they named the Truckee, in honor of the old Indian chief, who had piloted them to it.[28]

The cattle, not having eaten or drank for forty-eight hours, were almost famished. This march was of eighty miles[29] across an alkali desert, knee deep in alkali dust. The people, having water in their wagons, did not suffer so much, but there were occasions when it was extremely doubtful if they would be able to reach water with their cattle. So crazed were they with thirst that if the precaution had not been taken to unhitch them while yet some distance from the stream, they would have rushed headlong into the water and wrecked the wagons and destroyed their contents. There being fine grass and good water here, the party camped two days, until the cattle were thoroughly rested and refreshed.

Then commenced the ever-to-be-remembered journey up the Truckee to the summit of the Sierras. At first it was not discouraging. There was plenty of wood, water, grass, and game, and the weather was pleasant. The oxen were well rested, and for a few days good progress was made. Then the hills began to grow nearer together, and the country was so rough and broken that they frequently had to travel in the bed of the stream. The river was so crooked that one day they crossed it ten times in traveling a mile. This almost constant traveling in the water softened the hoofs of the oxen, while the rough stones in the bed of the river wore them down, until the cattle's feet were so sore that it became a torture for them to travel. The whole party were greatly fatigued by the incessant labor. But they dared not rest. It was near the middle of October, and a few light snows had already fallen, warning them of the imminent danger of being buried in the snow in the mountains. They pushed on, the route each day becoming more and more difficult. Each day the hills seemed to come nearer together and the stream to become more crooked.[30]

They were now compelled to travel altogether in the bed of the river, there not being room between its margin and the hills to furnish foothold to an ox. The feet of the cattle became so sore that the drivers were compelled to walk beside them in the water, or they could not be urged to take a step; and, in many instances, the teams had to be trebled in order to drag the wagons at all. On top of all these disheartening conditions came a fall of snow a foot deep, burying the grass from the reach of the cattle, and threatening them with starvation. The poor, foot-sore oxen, after toiling all day, would stand and bawl for food all night, in so piteous a manner that the emigrants would forget their own misery in their pity for their cattle. But there was nothing to offer them except a few pine leaves, which were of no effect in appeasing their hunger. Still the party toiled on, hoping soon to pass the summit and reach the plains beyond, and that beautiful land so eloquently described to them by Father Hookins. In face of all these obstacles, there was no thought of turning back. One day they came to some rushes that were too tall to be entirely covered by the snow; the cattle ate these so greedily that two of James Murphy's oxen died. However, by constant care in regulating the amount of this food, no evil effects were experienced, although it was not very nourishing. These rushes were scattered at irregular intervals along the river, and scouts were sent out each day to find them and locate a camp for the night. Some days the rushes would be found in a very short drive, and sometimes they would not be found at all.[31]

In this manner they dragged their slow course along until they reached a point where the river forked, the main stream bearing southwest and the tributary almost due west. Then arose the question as to which route should be taken. There being an open space and pretty good feed at the forks of the river, it was decided to go into camp and hold a consultation. This camp was made on what is now the site of the city of Truckee,[32] and the route pursued by these emigrants is practically that now followed by the Central Pacific Railroad. After considering the matter fully, it was decided that a few of the party should leave the wagons and follow the main stream, while the others should go by way of the tributary, as that seemed to be the more promising route for the vehicles.

Those who left the party were Mrs. Townsend, Miss Ellen Murphy, John Murphy, Daniel Murphy, Oliver Magnan, and Mrs. Townsend's servant, Francis. They each had a horse to ride, and they took with them two pack-horses and some provisions. The ladies had each a change of clothing and some blankets, and each man had a rifle and ammunition. There was still some game to be found, and as the Murphys were good hunters there was no thought of their starving. In our account of this journey we have followed the narrative of Mr. Schallenberger, who has kindly furnished us with the facts. In regard to this separation, John Murphy says that there was no consultation or agreement; that the persons spoken of were traveling in advance of the rest of the party, and, coming to the forks of the river, naturally took the main stream, expecting the others to follow, which they did not do. However this may be, the fact remains that the parties here separated and went the different routes as above stated.[33]

The party with the wagons proceeded up the tributary, or Little Truckee, a distance of two miles and a half,[34] when they came to the lake since known as Donner Lake. They now had but one mountain between them and California, but this seemed an impassable barrier. Several days were spent in attempts to find a pass, and finally the route, over which the present railroad is, was selected.[35] The oxen were so worn out that some of the party abandoned the attempt to get their wagons any further. Others determined to make another effort. Those who determined to bring their wagons were Martin Murphy, Jr., James Murphy, James Miller, Mr. Hitchcock, and old Mr. Martin, Mrs. James Murphy's father. The others left their wagons.

The snow on the mountains was now about two feet deep. Keeping their course on the north side of the lake until they reached its head, they started up the mountain. All the wagons were unloaded and the contents carried up the hill. Then the teams were doubled and the empty wagons were hauled up. When about half way up the mountain they came to a vertical rock about ten feet high. It seemed now that everything would have to be abandoned except what the men could carry on their backs. After a tedious search they found a rift in the rock, just about wide enough to allow one ox to pass at a time. Removing the yokes from the cattle, they managed to get them one by one through this chasm to the top of the rock. There the yokes were replaced, chains were fastened to the tongues of the wagons, and carried to the top of the rock, where the cattle were hitched to them. Then the men lifted at the wagons, while the cattle pulled at the chains, and by this ingenious device the vehicles were all, one by one, got across the barrier.[36]

After reaching the summit a drive of twenty miles westerly brought them to the head-waters of the Yuba River,[37] where the able-bodied men started for Sutter's Fort, then known as

New Helvetia, and now as the city of Sacramento. They walked and drove the cattle, expecting to return immediately with supplies for the train. The others remained in camp. Thus were the first wagons that ever made tracks in California soil, brought across the mountains.

Those who remained with the wagons on the Yuba were Mrs. Martin Murphy, with her four boys, Martin, James, Patrick W., and Bernard D.; Mrs. James Murphy, with her daughter Mary; Mr. James Miller, wife, and three children; Mrs. Patterson, with her children, and old Mr. Martin, Mrs. James Murphy's father. Leaving them here for the present, we will return to the wagons, which had been abandoned when the party divided at the forks of the Truckee.

Dr. Townsend and Mr. Schallenberger had brought with them an invoice of valuable goods, which they had intended to sell in California.[38] When the wagons were abandoned, Schallenberger volunteered to remain with them and protect the goods until the rest of the party could reach California and return with other and fresher animals with which to move them. Mr. Schallenberger thus describes his experience:—

"There seemed little danger to me in undertaking this. Game seemed to be abundant. We had seen a number of deer, and one of our party had killed a bear, so I had no fears of starvation. The Indians in that vicinity were poorly clad, and I therefore felt no anxiety in regard to them, as they probably would stay further south as long as cold weather lasted. Knowing that we were not far from California, and being unacquainted, except in a general way, with the climate, I did not suppose that the snow would at any time be more than two feet deep, nor that it would be on the ground continually.

"After I had decided to stay, Mr. Joseph Foster and Mr. Allen Montgomery[39] said they would stay with me, and so it was settled, and the rest of the party started across the mountains. They left us two cows, so worn out and poor that they could go no further. We did not care for them to leave us any cattle for food, for, as I said, there seemed to be plenty of game, and we were all good hunters, well furnished with ammunition, so we had no apprehension that we would not have plenty to eat, that is, plenty of meat. Bread we had not tasted for many weeks, and had no desire for it. We had used up all our supply of buffalo meat, and had been living on fresh beef and bacon, which seemed to satisfy us completely.

"The morning after the separation of our party, which we felt was only for a short time, Foster, Montgomery and myself set about making a cabin, for we determined to make ourselves as comfortable as possible, even if it was for a short time. We cut saplings and yoked up our poor cows and hauled them together. These we formed into a rude house, and covered it with rawhides and pine brush. The size was about twelve by fourteen feet. We made a chimney of logs eight or ten feet high, on the outside, and used some large stones for the jambs and back. We had no windows; neither was the house chinked or daubed, as is usual in log-houses, but we notched the logs down so close that they nearly or quite touched. A hole was cut for a door, which was never closed. We left it open in the day-time to give us light, and as we had plenty of good beds and bedding that had been left with the wagons, and were not afraid of burglars, we left it open at night also. This cabin is thus particularly described because it became historic, as being the residence of a portion of the ill-fated Donner party in 1846.[40]

"On the evening of the day we finished our little house it began to snow, and that night it fell to a depth of three feet. This prevented a hunt which we had in contemplation for the next day. It did not worry us much, however, for the weather was not at all cold, and we thought the snow would soon melt. But we were doomed to disappointment. A week passed, and instead of any snow going off more came. At last we were compelled to kill our cows, for the snow was so deep that they could not get around to eat. They were nothing but skin and bones, but we killed the poor things to keep them from starving to death. We hung them up on the north side of the house and covered them with pine brush. That night the meat froze, and as the weather was just cold enough to keep it frozen, it remained fresh without salt. It kept on snowing continually, and our little cabin was almost covered. It was now about the last of November or first of December, and we began to fear that we should all perish in the snow.

"The snow was so light and frosty that it would not bear us up, therefore we were not able to go out at all except to cut wood for the fire; and if that had not been near at hand I do not know what we should have done. None of us had ever seen snow-shoes, and of course had no idea how to make them, but finally Foster and Montgomery managed to make something they called a snow-shoe. I was only a boy and had no more idea of what a snow-shoe looked like than a Louisiana darkey. Their method of construction was this: Taking some of our wagon bows, which were of hickory and about half an inch thick, they bent them into an oblong shape forming a sort of hoop. This they filled with a network of rawhide.[41] We were now able to walk on the snow to bring in our wood, and that was about all there was to do. There was no game. We went out several times but never saw anything. What could we expect to find in ten feet of snow? It would sometimes thaw a little during the day and freeze at night, which made a crust on the snow sufficiently thick to bear the weight of a coyote, or a fox, and we used sometimes to see the tracks of these animals, but we were never fortunate enough to get a sight of the animals themselves.[42]

"We now began to feel very blue, for there seemed no possible hope for us. We had already eaten about half our meat, and with the snow on the ground getting deeper and deeper each day, there was no chance for game. Death, the fearful, agonizing death by starvation, literally stared us in the face. At last, after due consideration, we determined to start for California on foot. Accordingly we dried some of our beef, and each of us carrying ten pounds of meat, a pair of blankets, a rifle and ammunition, we set out on our perilous journey. Not knowing how to fasten snow-shoes to our feet made it very fatiguing to walk with them. We fastened them heel and toe, and thus had to lift the whole weight of the shoe at every step, and as the shoe would necessarily sink down somewhat, the snow would crumble in on top of it, and in a short time each shoe weighed about ten pounds.

"Foster and Montgomery were matured men, and could consequently stand a greater amount of hardship than I, who was still a growing boy with weak muscles and a huge appetite, both of which were being used in exactly the reverse order designed by nature. Consequently, when we reached the summit of the mountain about sunset that night, having traveled a distance of about fifteen miles,[43] I was scarcely able to drag one foot after the other. The day had been a hard one for us all, but particularly painful to me. The awkward manner in which our snow-shoes were fastened to our feet made the mere act of walking the hardest kind of work. In addition to this, about the middle of the afternoon I was seized with cramps. I fell down with them several times, and my companions had to wait for me, for it was impossible for me to move until the paroxysm had passed off. After each attack I would summon all my will power and press on, trying to keep up with the others. Towards evening, however, the attacks became more frequent and painful, and I could not walk more than fifty yards without stopping to rest.[44]

"When night came on we cut down a tree and with it built a fire on top of the snow. We then spread some pine brush for our beds, and after eating a little of our jerky and standing round our fire in a vain attempt to get warm, we laid down and tried to sleep. Although we were thoroughly exhausted, sleep would not come. Anxiety as to what might have been the fate of those who had preceded us, as well as uncertainty as to our fate, kept us awake all night. Every now and then one of us would rise to replenish the fire, which, though it kept us from freezing, could not make us comfortable. When daylight came we found that our fire had melted the snow in a circle of about fifteen feet in diameter, and had sunk to the ground a distance also of about fifteen feet.[45]

The fire was so far down that we could not get to it, but as we had nothing to cook, it made but little difference. We ate our jerky while we deliberated as to what we should do next. I was so stiff that I could hardly move, and my companions had grave doubts as to whether I could stand the journey. If I should give out they could afford me no assistance, and I would necessarily be left to perish in the snow. I fully realized the situation, and told them that I would return to the cabin and live as long as possible on the quarter of beef that was still there, and when it was all gone I would start out again alone for California. They reluctantly assented to my plan, and promised that if they ever got to California and it was possible to get back, they would return to my assistance.

"We did not say much at parting. Our hearts were too full for that. There was simply a warm clasp of the hand accompanied by the familiar word, 'Good-by,' which we all felt might be the last words we should ever speak to each other. The feeling of loneliness that came over me as the two men turned away I cannot express, though it will never be forgotten, while the, 'Good-by, Mose,' so sadly and reluctantly spoken, rings in my ears to-day. I desire to say here that both Foster and Montgomery were brave, warm-hearted men, and it was by no fault of theirs that I was thus left alone. It would only have made matters worse for either of them to remain with me, for the quarter of beef at the cabin would last me longer alone, and thus increase my chances of escape. While our decision was a sad one, it was the only one that could be made.[46]

"My companions had not been long out of sight before my spirits began to revive, and I began to think, like Micawber, that something might 'turn up.' [47] So I strapped on my blankets and dried beef, shouldered my gun, and began to retrace my steps to the cabin. It had frozen during the night and this enabled me to walk on our trail without the snowshoes. This was a great relief, but the exertion and sickness of the day before had so weakened me that I think I was never so tired in my life as when, just a little before dark, I came in sight of the cabin. The door-sill was only nine inches high, but I could not step over it without taking my hands to raise my leg. * * * [48] As soon as I was able to crawl around the next morning I put on my snow-shoes, and, taking my rifle, scoured the country thoroughly for foxes. The result was as I had expected—just as it had always been—plenty of tracks, but no fox.

"Discouraged and sick at heart, I came in from my fruitless search and prepared to pass another night of agony. As I put my gun in the corner, my eyes fell upon some steel traps that Captain Stevens had brought with him and left behind in his wagon. In an instant the thought flashed across my mind, 'If I can't shoot a coyote or fox, why not trap one.' There was inspiration in the thought, and my spirits began to rise immediately. The heads of the two cows I cut to pieces for bait, and, having raked the snow from some fallen trees, and found other sheltered places, I set my traps. That night I went to bed with a lighter heart, and was able to get some sleep.

"As soon as daylight came I was out to inspect the traps. I was anxious to see them and still I dreaded to look. After some hesitation I commenced the examination, and to my great delight I found in one of them a starved coyote. I soon had his hide off and his flesh roasted in a Dutch oven. I ate this meat, but it was horrible. I next tried boiling him, but it did not improve the flavor. I cooked him in every possible manner my imagination, spurred by hunger, could suggest, but could not get him into a condition where he could be eaten without revolting my stomach. But for three days this was all I had to eat. On the third night I caught two foxes. I roasted one of them, and the meat, though entirely devoid of fat, was delicious. I was so hungry that I could easily have eaten a fox at two meals, but I made one last me two days.

"I often took my gun and tried to find something to shoot, but in vain. Once I shot a crow that seemed to have got out of his latitude and stopped on a tree near the cabin. I stewed the crow, but it was difficult for me to decide which I liked best, crow or coyote.⁴⁹ I now gave my whole attention to trapping, having found how useless it was to hunt for game. I caught, on an average, a fox in two days, and every now and then a coyote. These last-named animals I carefully hung up under the brush shed on the north side of the cabin, but I never got hungry enough to eat one of them again. There were eleven hanging there when I came away. I never really suffered for something to eat, but was in almost continual anxiety for fear the supply would give out. For instance, as soon as one meal was finished I began to be distressed for fear I could not get another one. My only hope was that the supply of foxes would not become exhausted.

"One morning two of my traps contained foxes. Having killed one, I started for the other, but, before I could reach it, the fox had left his foot in the trap and started to run. I went as fast as I could to the cabin for my gun, and then followed him. He made for a creek about a hundred yards from the house, into which he plunged and swam across. He was scrambling up the opposite bank when I reached the creek. In my anxiety at the prospect of losing my breakfast, I had forgotten to remove a greasy wad that I usually kept in the muzzle of my gun to prevent it from rusting, and when I fired, the ball struck the snow about a foot above reynard's⁵⁰ back. I reloaded as rapidly as possible, and as the gun was one of the old-fashioned flint-locks that primed itself, it did not require much time. But, short as the time was, the fox had gone about forty yards when I shot him. Now the problem was to get him to camp. The water in the stream was about two and a half feet deep and icy cold. But I plunged in, and, on reaching the other side, waded for forty yards through the snow, into which I sank to my arms, secured my game, and returned the way I came. I relate this incident to illustrate how much affection I had for the fox. It is strange that I never craved anything to eat but good fat meat. For bread or vegetables I had no desire. Salt I had in plenty, but never used.⁵¹ I had just coffee enough for one cup, and that I saved for Christmas.

"My life was more miserable than I can describe. The daily struggle for life and the uncertainty under which I labored were very wearing. I was always worried and anxious, not about myself alone, but in regard to the fate of those who had gone forward. I would lie awake nights and think of these things, and revolve in my mind what I would do when the supply of foxes became exhausted. The quarter of beef I had not touched, and I resolved to dry it, and, when the foxes were all gone, to take my gun, blankets, and dried beef and follow in the footsteps of my former companions.

"Fortunately, I had a plenty of books, Dr. Townsend having brought out quite a library. I used often to read aloud, for I longed for some sound to break the oppressive stillness. For the same reason, I would talk aloud to myself. At night I built large fires and read by the light of the pine knots as late as possible, in order that I might sleep late the next morning, and thus cause the days to seem shorter.[52] What I wanted most was enough to eat, and the next thing I tried hardest to do was to kill time. I thought the snow would never leave the ground, and the few months I had been living here seemed years.

"One evening, a little before sunset, about the last of February, as I was standing a short distance from my cabin, I thought I could distinguish the form of a man moving towards me. I first thought it was an Indian, but very soon I recognized the familiar face of Dennis Martin. My feelings can be better imagined than described. He relieved my anxiety about those of our party who had gone forward with the wagons. They had all arrived safely in California and were then in camp on the Yuba. They were all safe, although some of them had suffered much from hunger. Mrs. Patterson and her children had eaten nothing for fourteen days but rawhides. Mr. Martin had brought a small amount of provisions on his back, which were shared among them. All the male portion of the party, except Foster and Montgomery, had joined Captain Sutter and gone to the Micheltorena war.[53] Dr. Townsend was surgeon of the corps. My sister, Mrs. Townsend, hearing that Mr. Martin was about to return to pilot the emigrants out of the wilderness, begged him to extend his journey a little farther and lend a helping hand to her brother Moses. He consented to do so, and here he was. Being a Canadian, he was accustomed to snow-shoes, and soon showed me how to fix mine so I could travel with less than half the labor. He made the shoe a little narrower, and fastened it to the foot only at the toe, thus making the heel a little heavier, so that the shoe would drag on the snow instead of having to be lifted at every step."

The next morning after Martin's arrival at the cabin he and Schallenberger started to return. Schallenberger's scanty diet and limited exercise rendered this a rather trying journey for him. But they arrived safely at the emigrants' camp, which, during Martin's absence, had been moved two days' journey down the hills. At this camp was born to Mr. and Mrs. Martin Murphy a daughter, the first white child born in California.[54] She was named Elizabeth, and afterwards married Mr. William Taaffe.

To make this history complete, we must return to the party which, separating from the wagons at the forks of the Truckee, followed the main stream. They continued up the river to Lake Tahoe, and were the first white people to look upon that beautiful body of water. Here they crossed the river, keeping on the west side of the lake for some distance, and then struck across the hills to the headwaters of the American River, which they followed down to the valley.[55] This route was exceedingly rough, much more so than the one up the Truckee on the other side. The American River was wider and deeper than the Truckee, and fully as crooked. They were compelled to cross it many times, and frequently their horses were compelled to swim, and the current was so swift as to make this a very hazardous undertaking. Mrs. Townsend rode an Indian pony, which was an excellent swimmer.[56] She would ride him across the river and then send him back by one of the boys for Ellen Murphy. Once this pony lost his feet. He had crossed the river several times and was nearly worn out. John Murphy had ridden him back to get a pack saddle, and on returning, the pony fell. John, though an excellent swimmer, had a narrow escape from drowning. The water was running with the force of a mill race, while the bed of the stream was full of huge rocks, against which he was dashed and disabled from swimming. The party on the banks were paralyzed with terror as he was swept down the raging torrent. Recovering themselves, they hurried down the stream, expecting at every step to see his mangled body thrown upon the shore. But John had not lost his head in his deadly peril. Watching his opportunity, as he was swept under a willow tree which grew on the bank, he seized the overhanging branches and held on with a death grip until he was rescued. The ice-cold water and the mauling he had received from the rocks rendered him unconscious. A warm fire restored him to his senses, but it was many days before he fully recovered from the shock caused by his involuntary bath.

The party were twenty-one days in getting to the valley. They did not suffer for food, for they were soon out of the snow and in a game country. John and Dan Murphy were excellent hunters, and there was no scarcity of meat. If game was scarce there was plenty of cattle roaming about, which made starvation impossible. They followed the American River until they came to St. Clair's ranch,[57] where they stopped for some time. Mr. and Mrs. St. Clair received them with a warm hospitality, which excited the liveliest feelings of gratitude in the hearts of the emigrants. These feelings were mingled with remorse when they thought of the number of St. Clair's calves that had been killed on the way down the river. They had, of course, intended to pay for them, but just at that time they had no money. The idea of accepting the hospitality of a man whose cattle they had killed, worked on their feelings until it nearly broke their hearts. The teachings of their father, the old patriarch, had kept their consciences tender, and they held many secret consultations as to what should be done in the premises.

They finally determined to confess. The lots cast for spokesman elected Dan Murphy, but it was agreed that all should be present to give him their moral support. Dan opened the interview by carelessly inquiring who owned all those calves that they had encountered coming down the river. St. Clair said he guessed they all belonged to him. "Well," said Dan, "there's a good bunch of them. What are calves about three months old worth in this country?" St. Clair told him. "Well," resumed Dan, "we killed some of them to eat, and we haven't got any money to pay you now, but if you will let us work out the price we will be very much obliged." The earnestness of the boys amused Mr. St. Clair very much, and when he told them that they were welcome to the calves they had killed, and as many more as they wanted to eat, they retired from the interview with a great load lifted from their consciences.

From St. Clair's they went down to Sutter's, arriving there about the same time that the men from the wagons got in. Here they found great excitement. Micheltorena had been appointed by the Mexican Government as Governor of California, with both civil and military authority. The former officials, Alvarado and Vallejo, had resolved to resist his authority, and had joined with them General Castro. The native Californians were very jealous of the foreigners, especially the immigrants from the United States. Taking advantage of this feeling, the revolutionists had roused the country and collected quite a formidable army. Whatever may have been the intention of the leaders, it was openly talked by the rank and file, that, after they had settled their difficulty with Micheltorena, they would drive the foreigners from the country. The Murphy party had not come two thousand miles across deserts and mountains to be driven back into the hills without an effort in their own defense, and without hesitation they joined a company that Captain Sutter was raising for the assistance of Micheltorena, who held the legal commission as Governor of California. With this company they went South, doing good service in the campaign as far as Santa Barbara. Here, there being no further need of their services, they started to return to their women and children, whom they had left with the wagons on the Yuba.

Here was another instance of the indomitable courage of these men. The whole country had been roused against Micheltorena and the foreigners, and here was a handful of these same foreigners who had been arrayed against them in every movement from the Sacramento to Santa Barbara, now returning alone through this hostile country with no protection but their trusty rifles. The boldness of the act was only equaled by the skill which enabled them to make the return journey without firing a hostile gun. It seems as if the hand of Providence had upheld them through all their tribulations and dangers, and preserved them for some great destiny.[58]

They arrived at the wagons about the same time that Schallenberger was rescued by Dennis Martin from his perilous situation in the cabin by Donner Lake. About the time Schallenberger joined the wagons, with Martin, a man named Neil, who had been sent by Captain Sutter, with a supply of provisions and horses, arrived at the camp.[59] The emigrants now were in a very cheerful frame of mind, being only one day's march from the plains, and the end of their year's journey in sight. The next day they pushed on, all mounted, some with saddles, some with pack-saddles, and some bare-back, and that night camped at the edge of the valley, on the banks of Bear River.[60] This was the first of March, just one year from the time they left Missouri. They found Bear River full and still rising, from the melting snow in the mountains and the heavy rainfall of the season. There was no bridge or ferry, and an attempt was made to find a tree of sufficient length to reach across, but in vain. In this search for a tree Mr. Neil, who had gone down the stream, was cut off from the mainland by the rapidly rising waters, leaving him on a little island, which was soon submerged, and as he could not swim, he was compelled to climb a tree.

His cries for help finally reached the ears of those in camp, and Schallenberger and John Murphy, each mounting a horse and leading a third one, swam into the foaming torrent and brought him safely to the shore.

Again the affairs of the emigrants began to assume a gloomy aspect. Bear River had overrun its banks until it was ten miles wide. The small supply of provisions sent in by Captain Sutter had been exhausted. Two deer had been killed, but this afforded scarcely a mouthful each to so large a party. There was no direction in which they could move except to return to the hills, and this would only be making their condition worse. Three days passed with no food. They could hear the lowing of the cattle across the river, and now and then could discern the graceful forms of herds of antelope on the other side of the water. Mr. Schallenberger relates an incident that occurred at this time. The Hon. B. D. Murphy was then a little chap only four years old.[61] As Schallenberger was sitting on a wagon-tongue, whittling a stick and meditating on the hollowness of all earthly things, and especially of the human stomach, little Barney approached him and asked if he would lend him his knife. "Certainly," replied Schallenberger, "but what do you want to do with it?" "I want to make a toothpick," said Barney. The idea of needing a toothpick when none of the party had tasted food for three days was so ridiculous that Schallenberger forgot the emptiness of his stomach and laughed heartily.

There was a large band of wild horses belonging to Captain Sutter, which were ranging in the foot-hills on that side of the river where the emigrants' camp was located. The question of killing one of these had been seriously discussed. The proposition had been earnestly opposed by Martin Murphy, who had declared that it was not food fit for human beings, and that although in the last stages of starvation his stomach would revolt at such diet. The respect that the young men had for Mr. Murphy restrained them from committing equicide for some time. But at last it became a question of horse meat or starvation.

One morning Mr. Murphy rode back over the trail to see if he could find any trace of an ox that they had lost on the march, while Schallenberger and Dennis Martin went hunting for something to eat. Returning empty handed, it was decided to kill a horse. Accordingly, Neil drove the band as near camp as possible, and Schallenberger shot a fine, fat two-year old filly. Mr. Murphy did not arrive until the meat had been dressed and was roasting before the fire. He had been unsuccessful in his search and was delighted to find that the boys had succeeded. With his face glowing with pleasure in anticipation of the feast, he inquired, "Who killed the heifer?" The party pointed to Schallenberger, and Mr. Murphy, patting him on the shoulder, exclaimed: "Good boy, good boy, but for you we might all have starved!" When the meat was cooked he ate of it, eloquently praising its juicy tenderness and fine flavor, which, he said, surpassed any meat he had ever tasted. About the time he had satisfied his appetite, his brother-in-law, James Miller, drew out the filly's mane from behind a log, exhibited it to Mr. Murphy, and asked him to see what queer horns they had taken from the heifer of which he had just been eating so heartily. Mr. Murphy's stomach immediately rebelled, and he returned to the ground the dinner which he had eaten with so much relish, saying, when he had recovered from his paroxysm, that he thought he had detected a peculiarly bad taste about that meat. He never, by any artifice, could be induced to taste horse flesh again.

Soon after this, the waters receded sufficiently to allow the party to reach Feather River, where, near Hick's Farm,[62] Captain Sutter had prepared a boat to ferry them across. Here the vaqueros brought them a fine fat cow, and, for the first time in many months, they had what Schallenberger called a "good square meal." [63]

Our pilgrims had reached the promised land. Their enduring faith had been lost[64] in sight, and their hopes had ended in fruition. The old patriarch had gathered his flock around him in the shadow of the Cross, in a country through the length and breadth of which the name of his family was destined to become a household word, and in the development and history of which they were to become prominent. Of all the property with which they started, little was left on their arrival in California. As Mrs. James Murphy said to the writer, "We brought very little property with us, but we did bring a good many days' work."

After a short rest at Sutter's Fort, the party separated, each to seek a location and to plant his roof tree in his adopted land.

Moses Schallenberger

The picture, from the San Jose *Pioneer* of April 15, 1893, shows Schallenberger presumably in his sixties.

Elisha Stevens

The picture, from the San Francisco *Daily Evening Post* of December 26, 1883, shows Stevens presumably as of that time; that is, at about the age of eighty.

1. *"They reached the summit of the Rocky Mountains."*

2. *"Westward over a broken country."*

3. "The party left the sink of the Humboldt."

4. "A desert lay before them."

5. "They reached a boiling spring."

6. "Here they halted two hours."

7. *"Across an alkali desert, knee deep in alkali dust."*

8. *"They frequently had to travel in the bed of the stream."*

9. *"One day they crossed it ten times in traveling a mile."*

10. *"Keeping their course to the north side of the lake."*

11. "They had now but one mountain between them and California."

12. "*We reached the summit of the mountain.*"

13. "*Twenty miles westerly brought them to the head-waters of the Yuba River.*"

14. "*Next day they pushed on.*"

Illustrations

1   "They reached the summit of the Rocky Mountains." The picture shows just about what the people of the Stevens Party must have seen as they looked back from this same point, near the Continental Divide, in July, 1844. The broad and quite undramatic nature of South Pass is impressive in this picture, as it was to the early travelers. The growth is typical sagebrush. In the distance appears the southern tip of the Wind River Mountains. The road shows the characteristic windings of an emigrant trail, and the wagons of the Stevens Party quite possibly went around these very curves. The road has never been graded. In 1844 it would have been much less sharply defined. The heavy covered-wagon traffic of later years, particularly in 1849, has worn it down about a foot below the general surface, as is emphasized by the late-afternoon shadow. (Picture taken in July, 1938.)

2   "Westward over a broken country." After leaving Raft River, the California trail threaded its way through many spectacular granitic formations, west of present Almo, Idaho. Schallenberger makes no mention of them, but many journal-keeping emigrants of later years expatiated on Pyramid Circle, or the City of Castles. The modern name has become the City of Rocks. Many emigrants carved or smoked their names on the smooth surfaces, and some of these names, with dates, are still decipherable. The large rock to the left, is now called The Kaiser's Helmet. On August 29, 1849, J. Goldsborough Bruff sketched it from just about the point at which the photograph was taken. (For his comments and a reproduction of his sketch, see *Gold Rush: The Journals . . . of J. Goldsborough Bruff*, ed. Georgia W. Reed and Ruth Gaines, New York, 1944, pp. 116-117.) Bruff mentions this rock as being to the left (i.e., of a man traveling westward) of the trail. Quite possibly therefore we may consider the present road as preserving the line of the trail, especially since no other route of travel can be observed in the neighborhood. On the other hand, certain considerations of terrain and the location of some inscriptions suggest that the trail may have kept to the right of both of these formations. (Picture taken in June, 1952.)

88   *The Opening of the California Trail*

3   "The party left the sink of the Humboldt." This is an aerial view of the Forty-Mile Desert, looking southeast from a point about three miles northeast of the hot springs. The highway is U. S. 40. The Desert Range is at the right; the Humboldt Range, at the left; the Stillwater Range, in the distance. Humboldt Sink is at the left under the low-lying cloud. This highly untypical cloud is the result of the recent heavy rains. The winding trail, merging with U. S. 40 at the right, is almost certainly the old emigrant road. The trace of this road can be followed most of the way across the Forty-Mile Desert. It no doubt was used to some extent until the automobile period, and may still be used occasionally. This quite possibly represents the actual trail broken through the sagebrush by the wagons of the Stevens Party in October, 1844. (Picture taken in November, 1950; reproduced also in my *U. S. 40.*)

4   "A desert lay before them." The view is westward from a low-flying plane. The hot spring in the middle of the Forty-Mile Desert shows as a white patch of steam near the center of the picture. The old emigrant trail may be seen in the foreground, curving in toward the spring. In the background toward the right it is marked by the reflection of water lying on it from recent rains, as it curves off to intersect the well-marked line of U. S. 40, thus avoiding the hill. After skirting the hill, the old trail bends to the left, and makes for the end of the well-marked ridge extending out into the plain. From the point of this ridge Picture 7 was taken. (Picture taken in November, 1950.)

5   "They reached a boiling spring." The view is in a westerly direction, from a low-flying plane. The picture shows the hot springs in the Forty-Mile Desert, and the main emigrant trail at the lower right. Note that it has been definitely worn down, showing heavy or long-continued traffic. Beyond the spring the trail shows a split, which unites at the top center. The older branch is probably the right-hand one, which closer to the spring has been wholly eroded by the small stream from the spring. The spring itself shows merely as steam. Because of the impregnation of the soil with minerals, there is little growth in the vicinity. (Picture taken in November, 1950.)

6   "Here they halted two hours." Since this close-up of the spring was taken in warm weather, no steam is showing. The desolate nature of the country in the vicinity is striking. The basin showing at the right represents a modern attempt

Illustrations 89

to impound the water. Because this was the only water in forty miles, it was an inevitable resting place for emigrant trains, and is mentioned in numerous journals. Later emigrants learned to send parties of horsemen ahead to impound the overflow of the spring in smaller basins where it could cool and become palatable for the oxen. (Picture taken in June, 1952.)

7   "An alkali desert, knee deep in alkali dust." Some miles west of the hot springs the emigrant trail crossed the bed of a dry lake, white with salt deposits. It was a particularly bad stretch, and was mentioned by many emigrants. A continuation of the same trail that appears in the other picture of the Forty-Mile Desert here shows about halfway between the telephone poles and U. S. 40. This is the natural point at which the emigrants would have passed, for here they would have cut as close as possible to the projecting point of the hill from which the picture was taken. The dark area which the trail crosses at the right would be marshy at some times of year, but probably not in autumn when the emigrant trains were passing. The faint roads showing in the foreground are maintenance roads for the pole line. (Picture taken in May, 1949.)

8   "They frequently had to travel in the bed of the stream." The picture is taken from the present U. S. 40, looking eastward, about a mile south of Floriston. This is the tightest place in the whole canyon of the Truckee and is presumably the place at which the emigrants were forced to travel "altogether in the bed of the river." U. S. 40 avoids this narrow passageway by making a wide detour. The railway has been put through by the blasting of a ledge out of the face of the slope. The old road showing at the right above the railway cannot be an emigrant trail because it too has been cut out of the slope. These slopes have been denuded by lumbering and fires; in 1844 there must have been a heavy growth of large pines. (Picture taken in August, 1952.)

9   "One day they crossed it ten times in traveling a mile." A picture taken from a low-flying plane here shows the exit from Truckee Canyon into Martis Valley, about four miles east of the town of Truckee. The view is toward the south. Truckee Airport shows at the right; Prosser Creek, in the right foreground. Although this cannot have been the spot where the Stevens Party was forced to cross the river ten times in one mile, the winding nature of the river is well displayed. U. S. 40 crosses only once in this stretch, and the railroad not at all;

but the emigrants probably had to cross four times, perhaps oftener. The route followed by a well-engineered railroad or highway was often in its primitive state impassable for covered-wagon emigrants who would have to turn aside for a single cliff or rock, or even for a large tree. One must remember that what appears from an airplane to be a very minor bank may actually be too high and steep for a wagon to sidle along. Emigrants could go up and down very steep slopes, but not sideways along them, because the wagons had a rather high center of gravity and tipping over sideways was a constant danger. As well as can be figured out from the conditions of terrain now existing after railroad- and road-construction, the wagons would have entered the area of the picture on the near bank, and would have had to cross once before reaching Prosser Creek. The next crossing, a difficult one because of steep banks on both sides, would have been at the point where the steep slope of basalt comes right down to the river. The third would have been near the house; the fourth, somewhat to the left of the present bridge. No sign of the emigrant road shows in the picture, for probably no wagons except those of the Stevens Party ever passed here. (Picture taken in November, 1950; reproduced also in my *U. S. 40*.)

10   "Keeping their course to the north side of the lake." The view is eastward from a position near the crest and somewhat to the south of U. S. 40. The cabin where Schallenberger spent the winter was among the trees about half a mile from the farther end of Donner Lake. The emigrants brought their wagons along the north side (left) of the lake. U. S. 40, where it rounds Windy Point, shows at the center of the picture, and runs off toward the left. The old road showing in the right foreground is pre-1925, but since it runs along the face of the cliff it cannot represent the route by which the emigrants brought their wagons up. In the middle ground at the right are the railroad snowsheds. The "old pass" is just at the snowsheds. The long granite slope, up which the emigrants probably took their wagons (see Picture 11), extends from the two telephone poles at the top of the old road, downward, to the left. (Picture taken in August, 1952.)

11   "They had now but one mountain between them and California." From near the top of the pass and a little south of U. S. 40 the view is southeast. Donner Peak rises in the background. The railway snowsheds and the approach to the "old

Illustrations 91

pass" are at the right center. Windy Point on U. S. 40 is in the lower left. The extremely forbidding nature of the country around Donner Pass is here manifest. We must also remember that the Stevens Party had the additional hazard of two feet of snow at the time of their crossing. The granite slope up which I believe them to have taken their wagons (see note 36) here shows clearly, from near the highway to a point close to the snowsheds. (Picture taken in August, 1952.)

12 "We reached the summit of the mountain." The view is here westward from a crag on the slope of Donner Peak. U. S. 40 is at the right; the railway, with its snowsheds, is in the center. The present highway crosses at a slightly higher point, and the true Donner Pass, the one used by the roads prior to 1925, appears at the left. Two old roads lead up to it from the right, but both of these are constructed along the sides of cliffs and so cannot be the emigrant trail. The top of the granite slope, mentioned in the two preceding pictures, is in the lower right, and therefore we may assume that the line of the emigrant trail is approximately that of the road to the left of the granite dome in the center. Farther on, the road winding through the pass must of necessity follow the line of the trail of 1844, for there is no other place for it to go. Since this is the summit of the mountain, we may assume that close to this point, perhaps in some location actually visible in the picture, Schallenberger and his two companions spent their miserable night in the deep snow and parted company in the morning. (Picture taken in September, 1949.)

13 "Twenty miles westerly brought them to the head-waters of the Yuba River." The trail is here seen as it descends westward toward a crossing of the Yuba River. The large rock in the center of the picture is also in the center of the road, and must have rolled in from above in recent years. There has also probably been a good deal of erosion along the line of the no-longer-used trail. The large rocks on both sides of the road bear the characteristic chocolate-brown markings which are iron oxide formed from particles of iron left from the scraping of wagon-tires. (Picture taken in October, 1945.)

14 "The next day they pushed on." From a plane the view here is south. The nearer canyon is Steep Hollow; the farther is the canyon of Bear River. The village of Dutch Flat, with its old gold diggings, lies in the middle distance. The general topographical nature of the foothill country is here manifest. The

ancient peneplain has been deeply channeled by the streams, but on the tops of the ridges the old, fairly smooth surface remains. The ridges therefore offer the only possible route for wagons. The emigrants of the Stevens Party followed this ridge between Bear River and Steep Hollow Creek from near Bear Valley until the uniting of the two streams. The curving road seen in the picture may be considered to represent this route. In many places the ridge is so narrow that the wagons could have passed nowhere else. When I first traveled this ridge, about 1933, the road was primitive, and it is still a dirt road. Even so, one must decide that in certain places it has been relocated from the original route. For instance, the emigrant road presumably must have gone right over the hump where the small white building (fire-lookout) now stands. Even in 1933, however, the road had been dug out around the side of the hill, with greater labor than the emigrants could have expended. (Picture taken in November, 1950.)

Notes

1   Cecilia Murphy identifies Father Hookins with Christian Hoecken, a priest active in western Missouri in the 'forties. In 1843 more was known about the location of California than Foote here states. Obviously he has tried to build up the Murphys. Still, it is true that no route for wagons was known.

    The religious motive, that is, the desire to escape to a Catholic country, such as California then was, is not much emphasized in connection with the Murphys.

2   The placing of Columbus second to the Murphys is probably the *ne plus ultra* of mug-book eulogy. The passage is also unfair, and even ridiculous, as regards Frémont, who arrived at Sutter's Fort on March 8, 1844, nine months before the first of the Stevens Party. Nevertheless, the author's points of comparison with Frémont's expedition are well taken. If we cannot place the men of the Stevens Party above Columbus, at least we may maintain that their achievement, entirely without government support, required more audacity and courage than that of Frémont, that it was perhaps more astutely executed, and that it was of more importance in establishing a route to California. It is of course highly unlikely that the Murphy family ever intended, as is here implied, to set forth on the journey by themselves. The fact that a party was being organized for California must have been noised about considerably in the western counties of Missouri during the winter of 1843-44.

3   Although Schallenberger is not mentioned until the third paragraph below, the Murphy material probably ends at this point. The date given in the next paragraph (March 1) is echoed by Schallenberger later on; apparently it was fixed in his mind as the date of departure from home.

4   The list is probably from Schallenberger, not from material supplied by the Murphys. We know (see "The Personnel") that Bancroft consulted Schallenberger as to the roster; moreover, Schallenberger's name occurs last, and this would be natural if he had compiled the list. The prominence given to the Murphys may be the result of a rearrangement by Foote.

So far as it can be checked, this list seems to be remarkably accurate. The only certain omission is that of the name of Edmund Bray.

5   This was Peter Sherreback. At least Bancroft so lists the name in his "Pioneer Register"; but he also declares that "it is written in a great variety of ways."

6   Schallenberger implies, I take it, that Stevens realized well enough what had happened, and was making only a *pro forma* investigation.

7   This river was the Elkhorn. Either Schallenberger was not quite sure of the name and so put it into quotation marks, or else he meant that it was to be taken as a kind of nickname. This use of quotation marks is, I think, another indication of his desire for accuracy in detail.

8   Derby is not included in the roster, and so was doubtless one of the emigrants for Oregon. He may have been the father of Perry Derby, who is mentioned later.

9   This statement about the pistols can be taken literally, for Montgomery was a gunsmith.

10 The figure of twenty-five miles represents a considerable underestimate. Even by air line it is about thirty-three miles. The necessity of breaking trail would also have held the party back. All in all, Hitchcock must have had a good deal of explaining to do. In the end, however, he was justified. By taking his advice, the party must have saved several days, and apparently did themselves no permanent harm. This cutoff immediately became an important route of travel. It is usually known as Greenwood's or Sublette's cutoff. For its connection with Greenwood, see "The Leadership," and "The Route." Since Bray mentions Hitchcock's association with the Sublettes, Hitchcock may have credited the cutoff to them, and its alternate name could have been thus established.

11 William Higgins appears in the *Call* list, which includes many of the Oregon company. Bean and Derby were also presumably Oregon emigrants. (See note 8.)

12 Thomas L. (Peg-leg) Smith was a well-known mountain man, especially famous for having amputated his own bullet-shattered leg with a butcher-knife. He and his post on Bear River are mentioned in many emigrant accounts.

Notes

13   The California Trail split from the Oregon Trail at Raft River, about two days' journey west of Fort Hall. The actual separation of the two parties, however, may have taken place at Fort Hall. The Oregon party, who were traveling over a known route, may have pushed off sooner, and the California party may have halted longer, for more careful preparation.

14   Although recognizing Stevens's captaincy, Schallenberger's part of the narrative nowhere gives a name to the party except at this point. As a title in *Pen Pictures* and in the opening paragraphs, which are certainly based upon information from the Murphys, the term "Murphy party" is used; Foote was thus committed and was unlikely to use any other term. I suspect that at this point Schallenberger originally wrote "the Townsend party," thus meaning to indicate not all the emigrants, but merely the Townsend family, together perhaps with their particular associates, such as the Montgomerys. Not liking to see the Murphys left out of it, Foote may have inserted the name. Or possibly Schallenberger may have meant to imply originally that both the Murphys and the Townsends were sufficiently supplied with food. The passage seems awkward, and some tampering is to be suspected.

15   As stated in "The Text," the reading should be "twenty-six men," not "twenty-six persons."

16   As stated in "The Route," the last sentence of the paragraph gives evidence of having been edited by Foote. The whole paragraph, in fact, is somewhat questionable. As evidence, the reader may check back over notes 14 and 15.

17   Although very brief, this description of the route is of the utmost importance. It shows that the Stevens Party followed the route of the later California Trail. Since we have already determined that they followed Walker's route of 1843, we may assume that it was he who established this part of the trail.

I have found no other record of Raft River being known as Beaver Creek, but that is such a common name that almost any stream might have been so called. Some miles east of Raft River, there was a stream known, in 1849 at least, as Beaver Dam Creek. Schallenberger may easily have confused the two, or Foote may have telescoped them carelessly in his editing.

The phrase "broken country" is well used of this sector, for here the emigrants threaded their way through the massive granite formations of the City of Rocks and then crossed the difficult Goose Creek Mountains. By "the head-waters of Mary's River" Schallenberger probably means the so-called wells, at the present site of Wells, Nevada. The route via Bishop Creek, which struck the Humboldt some ten miles farther west, was commonly used in 1849, but is probably a later development.

In passing, it might be mentioned that Walker, although he deserves high praise for having put the trail through, might have found a much better route for it. Modern highways have completely deserted this part of the old trail. In driving across it in the summer of 1952, I found the country almost as deserted as it must have been in 1843, and the roads almost as primitive. In fact, along much of Goose Creek the only track now existing does not even follow the route of the emigrant trail closely. Moreover, there does not seem to be any passable road at all that follows the trail over the ridge above the City of Rocks and across the Goose Creek Mountains. It is hard to see why Walker did not do as the modern route does: follow the line of the Oregon Trail about three days' journey farther west, and then turn south (along the line of present U. S. 93). He could thus have avoided the difficult country just mentioned, and there is no reason to think that problems of grass and water would have been any more difficult. The obvious explanation is, I think, pure ignorance on Walker's part. As I have said in the Introduction, we tend to exaggerate the geographical knowledge possessed by the early mountain men. The expression "he knew every foot of the West" is only a figure of speech.

A man always builds upon what knowledge he has already. Walker probably had traveled by the City of Rocks and Goose Creek route on horseback. He therefore took the wagons by the same way, believing it would be possible, even if not easy, to get them through. There was probably good beaver trapping in the high mountains just north of the City of Rocks, and for this reason the mountain men may have become familiar with this region. Possibly, also, there was already an established horse-trail from Fort Hall to the Humboldt by this route. We must note, however, that Walker sent his advance party of horsemen, not by this route, but "by way of Fort Boise . . . to the head of Pitt [sic] River, and thence down the Sacramento to Sutters Fort." *History of Napa and Lake Counties* (San Francisco, 1881), pp. 388-389. (See also J. C. Frémont, *Report, 1845,* under date of September 26, 1843.)

Notes

18 Schallenberger, like most pioneers, was no ethnologist. Under the term "Digger Indians" he seems to include both the Shoshones, or Goshiutes, and the Northern Paiutes. These two tribes, or groups of tribes, spoke different, although distantly related, languages. Since the Snakes were also Shoshones, Greenwood's "few words" should have been intelligible to them, but probably not to the Paiutes. The party would have encountered Goshiutes until close to the present site of Winnemucca.

19 These desert tribes were never very numerous, and we must raise an eyebrow at Schallenberger's "hundreds." Still, it must have seemed sometimes as if there were hundreds of them. Moreover, these Indians led a very hard life and were chronically hungry, and if there was any chance of a handout, the whole tribal population would quickly have turned out to be in on it.

20 "Five hundred miles" is another exaggeration. From Wells to Humboldt Sink by the present highway is not more than 275 miles, and the distance would not have been much greater by the emigrant road. Over-estimates of this kind, however, are only to be expected in covered-wagon narratives.

21 Schallenberger presents the situation with remarkable clarity, considering that he relied upon his recollections only. There is no mention of Walker's wheel-tracks; they must have led straight on toward the south. The doubt of the emigrants as to whether they should follow these tracks farther may have been the result of information that Walker had not been able to reach California with his wagons. (See "The Route.")

The country to the south, across Carson Sink, is so flat that it is now possible from any slight elevation, under good atmospheric conditions, to make out the trees along Carson River. Atmospheric conditions may not have been good during the week the Stevens party spent at Humboldt Sink, and Schallenberger mentions no attempt to explore southward. By going in that direction and then following up the Carson River the party might have done better for themselves than by doing as they did. Again we can only comment upon the comparative ignorance of the mountain men. There were three such men in the Stevens Party, but not one of them knew the geography surely at this point.

Quigley (pp. 200-201), apparently on the authority of Miller, presents an interesting picture of the life of the emigrants while encamped at the sink. "The cattle were let out to grass, the horses unharnessed, while the men and women, too, busied themselves with repairing outfits, mending damaged vehicles, washing soiled clothing, and the younger members busied themselves in shooting game, which, in the shape of wild ducks, geese, sage hens, as well as antelopes and deer, were very abundant, and scarely [sic] heeded the presence of their pursuers."

22   I cannot see how we can disregard Schallenberger's flat statement. (See also "The Leadership.") Guinn states: "Their pilot, Greenwood, was an old mountaineer and brought them safely to the sink of the Humboldt"; but his account is definitely less to be trusted than "Overland in 1844."

23   Truckee is a historical figure. He was the father of Winnemucca, and through him the grandfather of Sarah Winnemucca Hopkins. The family seems to have possessed intelligence and ability. Since Truckee was a Paiute, Greenwood's knowledge of Shoshone would probably have been of no use to him, and Truckee's facility at grasping the idea of what was wanted and then expressing himself by means of a diagram are the more remarkable. He must have drawn a map, or at least understood the significance of one that Greenwood drew in the sand, although he had never seen a book or a map in his life.

24   Except for mentioning March 1 at the beginning, this is Schallenberger's first date. From this point on, he gives some approximate dates, which generally turn out to be about correct, when they can be checked.

25   The build-up about John Greenwood leads to nothing, and may indicate an omission by the editor. In 1845 John Greenwood achieved his ambition and killed an Indian, in cold blood. W. F. Swasey, *The Early Days and Men of California,* pp. 32-33. (See also [Simeon Ide], *A Biographical Sketch of the Life of William B. Ide* [Claremont, N.H., 1880], p. 35, and Fred Lockley, *Across the Plains by Prairie Schooner,* Eugene, Ore. [n.d.], pp. 8-9.)

26   The mention of a "short feather blanket" is an indication of Schallenberger's accuracy. This sort of garment was worn by the Northern Paiutes.

27   The original line of the railroad passed close to these springs, although the present line does not. In spite of being well known since 1844, the springs have never really acquired a name. They are mentioned occasionally as Emigrant Springs, and recently

Notes

the proprietor of the gas-station there has put up the sign "Brady's Hot Springs." On the official highway map of Nevada, however, they still appear merely as Hot Springs. This is an interesting point in nomenclature, that in a state where there are many hot springs this particular one should have remained undistinguished. Probably this is because there is no other one at all near, and this one could definitely remain the Hot Springs. The water is not poisonous. The oxen may have become sick by drinking too much of it while it was still warm.

28 Different versions of the Truckee story have been told, but I see no reason to doubt the essential accuracy of this one. It is accepted by Erwin G. Gudde in his *California Place Names*. According to Mrs. Hopkins, who was in a position to know, Truckee was not his name at all: "Truckee is an Indian word, it means *all right,* or *very well.*" He apparently used this expression so frequently that the emigrants took it to be his name.

Near the Truckee the emigrants must have crossed Frémont's trail, about nine months old and marked not only by the passage of many horses but also by the wheelmarks where the famous howitzer had been hauled. No reminiscence makes any mention of this trail. At the moment, the emigrants had many other things on their minds, and so the trail probably made little impression upon them and was afterward forgotten.

29 "Eighty miles" is a great overestimate. Although we cannot be sure from just what point the Stevens Party took off, the distance was probably not much more than forty miles. It was later ascertained more accurately, and this region is still known as the Forty-Mile Desert.

Bray states: "the morning we started had a severe gale and some snow, which drove us back to camp." A snow flurry would be easily possible in that area in October. Even if Schallenberger had forgotten this false start, it might have built up in him the general idea of difficulty and greater distance.

30 The "journey up the Truckee" obviously made a tremendous impression upon Schallenberger, and he remembered many details. It is doubtful, however, whether he remembered the sequence of events very clearly. He does not, for instance, distinguish between Lower Truckee Canyon, and Upper Truckee Canyon, with the intervening level stretch of Truckee Meadows, where Reno now is located.

The distance traveled up the river is only about seventy miles by the modern highway, and cannot have been much longer by the emigrant road. My tentative dates indicate that the party began this journey (from the site of present Wadsworth) on October 12, and arrived at the forks on November 14. This would make a total of thirty-four days, with an average rate of travel of about two miles a day. In other words, the wagon-train was practically stalled, and only by the very greatest effort could the party move at all. The statement "for a few days good progress was made" must therefore be taken in a relative sense only. Good progress for a wagon-train would mean at least twelve miles a day, and such a rate would have taken the party clear to Truckee Meadows in three days. But even the lower canyon was extremely hard, and accounts of later emigrants, such as those of the Donner Party, are eloquent about its difficulties. The upper canyon was even harder, and so far as is known, no other emigrants took wagons through it.

I have attempted, on the ground, to work out the points where the curving of the river forced the emigrants to cross. The worst part of the canyon is in the vicinity of Floriston, and it was here probably that the emigrants were forced to travel "altogether in the bed of the river." The lower canyon is not so tight, and I have difficulty in making out the points where so many crossings would have been necessary. Something to remember is that originally the riverbanks may have been thickly grown with cottonwood and willow, and that the emigrants would sometimes have saved time and energy by making another crossing rather than by cutting out a passageway.

The reminiscences of the Donner Party (1846) mention forty-nine crossings from Wadsworth to Verdi. This number is perhaps an exaggeration. Bryant makes it "about thirty" and Jefferson's map shows twenty-five. Bryant, however, was on horseback and may have avoided some of the crossings, and Jefferson may merely have marked as many as he could get on his map.

31 A variety of rush is a characteristic growth around springs in Nevada. I have noticed it at one spot along Truckee River, but it could probably have been found at other places in early times, especially in the vicinity of springs. It is possible also that some of these "rushes" were actually bunches of tall, dry rye-grass, which could easily have stood up above the snow.

32 The "point where the river forked" is the junction of Donner Creek with the Truckee. When Schallenberger refers to the smaller stream as the "Little Truckee," he does not mean

the stream which is at present so called. The camp was only approximately "on what is now the site of the city of Truckee," if it was made where the stream forked. The fork is about a mile west of the town.

Schallenberger is not exact about his compass-bearings, but he is certainly as exact as could be expected after forty years.

33 The difference of opinion between Schallenberger and John Murphy as to the reason for the separation of the two parties is difficult to understand. John Murphy was a member of the horseback party; Schallenberger should have been present when the emigrants were "considering the matter fully" and should have got good information from his sister, who was also a member of the horseback party. Since there is no sure evidence to show which opinion is actually correct, we can only work from likelihood.

On this point, as generally, I find Schallenberger's opinion reasonable. We may consider the circumstances: (1) The horseback party was a group of young men and women, only one of them married. They were thus the kind of people who would naturally be picked for a detached party. (2) They are described as well-equipped—pack-horses, food, rifles and ammunition, blankets—and indeed they would have had to be so equipped to get through at all.

If we accept Murphy's idea, we have to assume that this picked group, all equipped for independent action and rapid travel, "just happened" to be riding in advance of the others, to follow the main stream, and then to continue going without even attempting to find out what had happened to the main party. This is more than I am ready to believe as being mere accident.

There is another possibility. Can this have been a calculated desertion? Did the six prepare in advance, and deliberately leave the others in the lurch? Such action might readily be imagined of Magnent and Deland ("Mrs. Townsend's servant"). These two had no family ties and can have had few bonds of loyalty to the party. But I think it wholly unlikely that Mrs. Townsend, an estimable woman by all accounts, would have deserted her husband and brother, or that the three young Murphys, members of a tightly knit family, would thus have left their father and other kinsfolk.

On the whole, therefore, I hold with Schallenberger, although it is difficult to see how John Murphy could have become so badly confused, or why he should have invented a story. In

Chronicles of the Builders, although it usually favors Murphy sources, John Murphy's idea is not mentioned.

The horseback party—by its composition, equipment, and route taken—thus suggests to me not anything accidental but on the contrary a deliberately calculated and quite reasonable expedient to double the chances that at least some of the emigrants would get through to Sutter's Fort and from that base be able to bring or send help to the others, if this was needed.

34   The distance here is about correct. It would be at least two miles.

35   By "the route, over which the present railroad is," Schallenberger obviously means that the emigrants crossed at Donner Pass. He does not intend to imply that they followed the whole route of the railroad, for he specifically mentions that they kept "on the north side of the lake." This point is important, for many have assumed that the original crossing of the Sierra was via the head of Cold Creek.

This route is confirmed for 1845 by *A Biographical Sketch of the Life of William B. Ide,* and for early 1846 by Edwin Bryant's *What I Saw in California.* T. H. Jefferson's map (*op. cit.*) shows the Schallenberger cabin but not Donner Lake, and so probably indicates that by late 1846 the trail had been relocated, or at least that there was an alternate trail.

36   At various times in the last twenty years I have scrambled up and down Donner Pass, trying—on the whole, unsuccessfully—to discover traces of the old road. I still think that it may be done, but I am getting old for that kind of research, and leave the project to my youngers, wishing them "Good hunting!" The trouble is that the construction of the railroad and more recent roads, to say nothing of pole lines, has changed the face of things. There has been a great deal of blasting and grading. I have never been able even to locate the vertical rock-wall mentioned in the text.

I venture to say only a little. About a half-mile west of the lake is a small meadow. This would have been a likely location for a base camp. At the other end, almost at the top of the pass (about two hundred yards down the road from the observation point, and just west of the bend known as Windy Point) there is a long slope of bare granite. It would be possible to haul wagons up this slope, and they would thus have been heading directly for the lowest spot of the pass. (This is the actual pass, and was used by the old highway.) On this granite slope are a few of the characteristic rust marks left by wagon-tires on granite. I believe therefore that at some time wagons were hauled up here. Since the Stevens Party crossed in snow, their wagons would probably not have left marks on the granite, but such marks may have been left by the wagons of later parties.

37   Technically speaking, the wagons came "to the head-waters of the Yuba River," as soon as they crossed the watershed of the pass. The statement that they did not come to the headwaters of that river until they were twenty miles west of the pass is thus evidence that the Stevens Party established the route of the later emigrant road. This route kept to the ridge to the south of the river, and then came down to it, by what was known later as Devil's Hill, at Hampshire Rocks, actually about twenty miles from the pass. The Yuba River camp I believe to have been slightly farther on, at the present campground near Big Bend Ranger Station. The evidence is that Jefferson's map (*op. cit.*) shows a house beyond the second crossing of the Yuba, which should be just about at the place mentioned. Jefferson records the road as of 1846, and it is unlikely that any other house had been built near here in that short interval.

A few details of occurrences at this camp are given by Quigley (pp. 202-205), apparently from reminiscences of Miller, who is made the hero.

38   In *Chronicles of the Builders* (III, 31) it is stated that Townsend's wagon contained "an invoice of costly goods consisting of broadcloth satins and silks." Although the source is not the best, such materials would have been a reasonable cargo to expect, being light and valuable, and being in demand in California.

39   Montgomery was a close associate of Dr. Townsend's, and had been Schallenberger's companion on one of the buffalo hunts. Foster had accompanied Stevens and Townsend in scouting ahead across the Forty-Mile Desert. His willingness to stay at the lake may indicate that he too had a wagon to watch.

40   Edwin Bryant saw the cabin on August 25, 1846, and does it the compliment of describing it as "a tolerably well-constructed log-house." In the litter with which the floor was strewn, Bryant picked up an envelope addressed to "Dr. John Townsend, Bloomfield, Ind." (See *What I Saw in California*, under date given.)

The site of the cabin was close to the present Donner Monument, but not exactly at that point. (The monument was placed at the center of a small plot of land reserved for it.) In 1846 the Breen family occupied this cabin, and Keseberg built a kind of lean-to against it for his family. Some of his cannibalistic exploits presumably took place here. On June 22, 1847, after various remnants of human bodies had been collected and buried, the cabin was burned by order of Major Thomas Swords, apparently as a kind of purification ceremony.

41   Members of the Donner Party, similarly trapped in 1846, made frames for snowshoes by sawing oxbows into thin strips. Which was the better method, I am unable to state. Neither kind of snowshoe seems to have worked at all well. The trouble, however, was due not wholly to the snowshoes themselves, but largely to the nature of the snow. Snow in the Sierra Nevada is very often sticky, and skis are usually preferable to snowshoes.

42   As regards the more important animal life, the situation that winter may be described about as follows. The bears had gone into hibernation. The native trout in the lake were in a semi-hibernating condition, and would not have responded to a hook readily, even if one could have been lowered to them through the ice and snow. The deer had descended to less snowy altitudes. Rabbits and grouse were undoubtedly still active, but kept to the bases of fir trees where the down-sloping branches act like a roof and keep a small area free from snow. The rabbits and grouse were living largely on spruce buds, and rarely came out to leave tracks on the snow. Accordingly, a greenhorn like Schallenberger may not even have known that they were there. Foxes and coyotes were living on the rabbits and grouse. During the time of heavy storms the foxes and coyotes probably were unable to get around in the very soft snow, and so holed up. The crow—since it was solitary, it may have been a raven—was probably just around and about, after the nature of crows and ravens, to see what it could pick up. The Washoe Indians, like the deer, had returned to lower levels to get out of the snow. Guinn states that Schallenberger's first fox was a black one.

43   Schallenberger's much later reference to Christmas makes it likely that this snowshoe journey was considerably earlier in December. I would put it roughly about the middle of the month. "About fifteen miles" is again a great exaggeration,

Notes

but is not to be wondered at, under the circumstances. The actual distance is about six miles.

44   If these cramps were in the legs, as seems likely, they may have been partly the result of the unusual method of walking necessitated by the snowshoes. Also, they may have resulted from a deficiency in the diet. Schallenberger had probably had little milk in the last few months and may have been suffering from malnutrition in various ways. To a still-growing boy such lacks would have been much more serious than to the older men.

45   The regular method for building a fire on top of deep snow was to cut a green tree, chop it into logs, and make a platform of these logs. On top of this platform a fire was built of dry wood obtained from a dead tree. Whether Schallenberger and his companions knew this method, or merely improvised, is not certain. Their experience of having the fire melt a deep hole into the snow is paralleled by that of some of the Donner Party, in March, 1847, near this same spot.

46   At this point Foster and Montgomery disappear from the narrative, except for the statement that they did not join Sutter's forces. By negative inference, since no comment is made anywhere on their snowshoe journey, we can assume that it was not outstandingly difficult. They are not mentioned as participating in the final relief party, or as ever trying to help Schallenberger. We cannot, however, decide much on mere lack of evidence. Schallenberger himself seems to have held no resentment against them.

47   Schallenberger cannot have thought of Mr. Micawber at this particular time, or have read of him at the lake, for *David Copperfield* was not published until 1849-50. The absence of literary allusions indicates that Schallenberger was not usually much of a reader. I have been able to spot only a vague and commonplace Biblical reference: "in sight of the promised land." The comparison to "the quills on the back of a porcupine" is probably proverbial or from nature, not a reminiscence of "the fretful porpentine" of *Hamlet*.

Along with the lack of references to the Bible one should note also the absence of religious feeling. One emergency calls forth: "trusting to Providence." Another mention of Providence is in a passage that is presumably Foote's.

48   See "The Text," for comment on the asterisks. Possibly Schallenberger, weak and exhausted, was seized with some kind of disagreeable physical symptoms which Foote thought better to omit.

49   The preference for fox over coyote would not be expected a priori. I admit that I have not tested the matter by personal experiment, and I have not even talked with anyone who has eaten either fox or coyote. An interesting article by Martin Schmitt, " 'Meat's Meat': An Account of the Flesh-eating Habits of Western Americans" (*Western Folklore*, XI [July, 1952], pp. 185-203), fails to give much help on this particular point. In his list of "creatures 'not usually eatable,' but fair game for a hungry man" Schmitt includes both fox and coyote. He fails to have a special entry for fox, but for coyote gives two paragraphs indicating that it is likely to be pretty bad. However, wolf-meat (which he admits might be coyote) receives several favorable comments. Moreover, Indians, and white men who associated with them, frequently ate dog meat and considered it a delicacy, and a coyote is not much different from an Indian dog. My own opinion is that Schallenberger, to begin with, was unlucky enough to trap a very old and tough coyote. A young coyote, in good condition, ought to be just as edible as any fox.

As for a crow, the phrase "eating crow" is a synonym for degradation and hardship. Moreover, John Lewis Manly (see his *Death Valley in '49*, San Jose, 1894) tried crow, and his experience fully corroborates that of Schallenberger. Schmitt, however, is less misocoracous.

50   The use of "reynard's" is one of the few flourishes of diction to be observed in the narrative, except where we may suspect that the wording is Foote's.

51   The failure to use salt is curious, but there is a considerable human variation in taste for salt. Since he was living on a wholly flesh diet, Schallenberger would probably obtain a sufficiency of salt from the flesh itself.

52   An article in the *Pony Express* (September, 1946), accompanying a portrait of Schallenberger states: "His favorite reading material during that long winter was *Lord Chesterfield's Letters to His Son* and the works of Byron." Since Schallenberger's daughters, then living, are thanked for the portrait, we may suppose that they also supplied the information about

the books, and that this information came to them from their father.

53   For comment on "the Micheltorena war" and the participation of the members of the Stevens Party, see note 58.

54   The statement, taken literally, would mean that the baby was born in the camp that was two days' journey from the original camp. This is possible, but most other evidence suggests the contrary. Bray makes it appear that the baby was born very soon after the arrival at the first camp. Mrs. Murphy's being taken in labor may therefore have forced a halt; once halted, the train was snowed in. The statement that this was "the first white child born in California" is ridiculous.

The baby was called Elizabeth Yuba Murphy, a name to be compared with that of Ellen Independence Miller, who was born near Independence Rock. *Chronicles of the Builders* (III, 39) states that she later married "William P. Taaffe, one of the leading merchants of San Francisco."

55   Although we have no further information about the route of the horseback party except the scanty data here preserved, the necessities of geography allow us to follow them with an accuracy not to be ordinarily expected. They went up along the Truckee River and at the time of reaching the lake were on the east bank. They crossed the river, and kept on the west side "for some distance." As for the stream along which they ascended from the lake, we may consider Ward Creek, Blackwood Creek, and McKinney Creek. McKinney Creek is the most likely. Its distance from the river, about seven miles, satisfies the description. The pass at its head is 7,142 feet, about the same height as Donner Pass, and the party should have had no difficulty in taking horses across it. To have done so at the head of either of the other creeks would have been difficult, if not impossible, and we should therefore expect some mention even in a brief record. As it is, the crossing of the pass is not really mentioned at all, and all that is said is that they then "struck across the hills."

If they crossed by the head of McKinney Creek, they would have come to the headwaters of the American River. As a matter of fact, they would also have done so if they had crossed by either of the other creeks.

From the head of McKinney Creek, they would have descended almost immediately a thousand feet. From that point on, they followed the water downward. Although this route beside the river would certainly have been "exceedingly rough," it is possible for people on horseback, and it had the great advantage of bringing them quickly to a moderate altitude, and thus out of the snow. In a distance of only about ten miles from the top of the pass they would have descended to an altitude of about 4,500 feet. As the narrative states: "they were soon out of the snow." At 4,500 feet there would probably have been no snow until after the big storm that began on November 28 or thereabouts. By that time the horseback party should have been at a still lower altitude.

The water "which they followed down to the valley" would have been the Rubicon River, the Middle Fork of the American River, the North Fork, and finally the main stream. The American River was probably the only name by which any of these streams was known in 1844.

Frémont had seen the lake from the mountains on February 14, 1844, only nine months earlier. In all probability, however, this group of six were the first white people ever actually to reach Lake Tahoe. In *Chronicles of the Builders* Daniel Murphy is said to have been riding "some miles" in advance, and thus to have been the first to arrive at the lake. Why he should have been riding so far ahead is difficult to conceive, but there is no reason why he should not have been "the first." We should remember, however, that the statement occurs in a strongly pro-Murphy source.

56 We should note with interest that Mrs. Townsend had the Indian pony. According to all accounts, Dr. Townsend was just the kind of man who would trade horses. The narrative notes the attaining of some ponies at Fort Laramie, and also some from "Peg-leg" Smith; apparently these transactions paid off.

57 John Sinclair (as the name is more commonly spelled) was living at his ranch a few miles north of Sutter's Fort. (For the date at which the horseback party arrived there, see "The Chronology.") Since John Murphy was a member of this party, he may have supplied some of the material for this section, particularly the details about the killing of the calves, which Mrs. Townsend might not have thought worth passing on to Schallenberger. We should notice, however, that on one occasion the point of view is not John Murphy's. "The party on the banks were paralyzed with terror" does not sound like

anything he would have thought about at the time or would have wanted to report later.

58 One of the most puzzling problems in connection with the whole story is the apparent desertion of the women and children and the subsequent involvement of the men in a California revolution. I shall attempt to present the situation.

Having got the wagons to the top of the pass about November 25, the party would have managed to get to the site of their Yuba River camp when the big storm struck, about November 28. Perhaps at this time also, as I have suggested in note 54, Mrs. Murphy was taken in labor. Here, according to Quigley (p. 202), "log-cabins were built, all of the cattle that was not needed for work around the camp or used by the men to go in search of relief, were killed, and the flesh carefully preserved for the subsistence of those in camp." Bray states: "After a weeks delay 8 of us started with pack oxen leaving the women and children under the charge of James Miller, with the starved oxen for food and the waggons for shelter, leaving the women & children was a sad alternative, but it was under the circumstances the best thing to be done." Bray may be right that this was "the best thing to be done," but in several details he creates confusion. He implies that no cabin was built; actually, Miller and "old man" Martin may have done the building later. Bray, however, does not mention Martin as being left behind, although Schallenberger does. Seventeen, not eight men, must have left the camp, but possibly they went in two sections, and Bray remembered the numbers of only his own group.

Bray continues: "We made the best of our way without a guide [note that he again recalls no help from Greenwood] and arrived at Johnson's Ranch on Bear River on the 23rd Dec. We camped at Nicholas and the next morning came on to John Sinclairs." Bray is here using later names. By "Johnson's Ranch" he must mean the site of the ranch; and by "Nicholas," the ranch of Nicholaus Allgeier, the present Nicolaus. As usual, also, he is too late in his date, as shown by Sutter's letter of December 15. Actually, their week at the Yuba River should have been about November 29–December 5. If they left there about December 6, this would allow them a reasonable length of time to arrive at Sutter's on December 13, allowing for snow and the troublesome task of driving pack-oxen.

There is no need here to go into the whole background of the Micheltorena affair. An account of it may be found in Bancroft, Vol. IV, chap. xxi. Suffice it to say that the men of the Stevens Party came at Sutter's Fort into a hotbed of revolution, and counter-revolution. At the moment, Sutter was raising troops, and was about to cast the die in what he must have considered a desperate gamble. Twenty-one riflemen suddenly descending from the mountains would have seemed to him a heaven-sent reinforcement. To get them to join his ranks, he could entice and he could threaten. He may have held from the governor, and he certainly had forces to exercise, the power of conscription. To be sure, our narrative states that the men enlisted "without hesitation," but the language of this passage is suggestive of the editor, who was given to bombast, and elsewhere coercion is suggested (see Bancroft, IV, 486, n.).

On the other hand, Sutter would probably have promised to send help to the women, and he might even have pointed out that they would be safer in the mountains than if exposed to the hazards of war.

In one way or another, the matter was accomplished. The names of several who went with the company are listed by Bancroft (IV, 486, n.), and some others are given elsewhere, so that there is no need to doubt the accuracy of the statement in the narrative: "all the male portion of the party, except Foster and Montgomery had joined Captain Sutter," except obviously to qualify by noting that Schallenberger was still at the lake and that Miller and probably "old man" Martin were with the women and children.

On January 1 the little army left Sutter's Fort. Dr. Townsend was an officer, serving as surgeon (according to our narrative), or as aide-de-camp (according to Bancroft and other accounts). Doubtless he acted in both capacities. The other twenty, whether willing or not, rode in the ranks of Gantt's mounted riflemen.

Having joined the governor and his Mexican battalion, they all started south from Salinas on January 13. Micheltorena was suffering from a severe case of the piles. He could not ride a horse at all, and could not even go very far in a carriage. Progress was correspondingly slow, and the force finally reached Santa Barbara early in February.

By this time, the Americans were getting restless and disgusted. Some of them were deserting—although such a military word should scarcely be used to describe going over the hill from such a rag-tag organization as this. Among others who must have "left" about this time we can name Dennis Martin,

John Murphy, and Martin Murphy, Jr. Dennis Martin, we know, got to Donner Lake on a day which can scarcely have been later than February 26. To do so, on horseback and afoot, in addition to collecting provisions and making snowshoes, I would figure twelve days as the absolute minimum, and would much rather allow several days more. *Chronicles of the Builders* (III, 37) has John Murphy leaving Santa Barbara about February 17, but either this date is too late or Martin left before John Murphy.

Martin Murphy, Jr., is the only other emigrant besides Martin and John Murphy mentioned by Schallenberger as having participated in the relief party, but there is no statement as to there being no others.

Chronicles of the Builders indicates that John Murphy was taken prisoner and paroled, and that then "the Murphys" were granted permission to go to the relief of the families. We must remember that Sutter, who was generally humanitarian and no tyrant, may have found that his conscience was bothering him at the thought of the women and children left marooned. Also, he may have found that the same thought was destroying the morale of his force. If so, he would have been likely to allow the men to go on this mission, and to have forwarded instructions for relief to be sent from the fort. This would account more literally for the statement that Neal was "sent by Captain Sutter."

We may, therefore, reconstruct about what happened. The party rode north as fast as possible, backtracking. There is no reason to believe that this ride was at all dangerous or that its safe completion called for any special care of Providence, as the text (doubtless, the editor) declares. At the fort they delivered Sutter's letter, or else persuaded whoever was left in charge there to send relief to those still with the wagons. If persuasion was not enough, they probably threatened. Mrs. Townsend used this opportunity to speak to Martin about her brother.

Apparently snow conditions were not bad at this time, and the relief party does not seem to have had a difficult time in getting through. On the way, they met Miller and his son, who were coming out to get food and make contact. (See Quigley, p. 204.) Martin, being a Canadian, was probably skilled on snowshoes, and so got through to the lake easily.

The rest of the mock-heroic campaign, together with how some of the Murphys were taken prisoner, and what the Americans did at the great battle of Cahuenga—behold, are they not written in the histories of California? It is told, moreover, that when one of the Murphys returned from that campaign, he did not even have a pair of pants, but was riding his horse draped in a blanket.

59 Both Samuel Neal and John Neal (so spelled in Bancroft's "Pioneer Register") worked for Sutter. It is difficult, and quite unimportant, to determine which is here meant.

60 "At the edge of the valley," on what was obviously the north bank of Bear River, the emigrants must have been at what was later the site of Johnson's ranch. Unfortunately for the emigrants, Johnson did not settle there until later in this same year.

61 B. D. Murphy rose to be state senator and mayor of San Jose, and so is here referred to as "the Honorable."

62 Sutter's Hock Farm, which is obviously meant, was on the west bank of the Feather River, almost directly west of the point at which the emigrants had emerged from the mountains.

63 Schallenberger's narrative apparently ends at this point. We are fortunate, however, in being able to supply an ending from Guinn: "With Pat Martin he [Schallenberger] remained at the fort until June and then returned to guard the wagons, with their valuable stock of merchandise . . . Meanwhile the snow had vanished from the lake and the Indians had found the wagons and the cabin, from which they had removed everything but the guns and ammunition. It is probable that they were unused to such equipments and feared to touch them. In July the oxen arrived and the wagons were taken to California, being the first that ever were brought into the state. In his possession Mr. Schallenberger still has a wheel tire which he prizes as a souvenir of the eventful trip." (This is confirmed by "Letters from California" signed "The Farthest West," in *Magazine of History*, Vol. XXIV, No. 2, p. 8.)

64 Something has gone wrong. Probably we should read "kept" instead of "lost."

Bibliographical Note

Except for Schallenberger's memoirs the materials on the Stevens Party are scanty and generally inaccurate. Bancroft in his *History of California* (see below) lists what was available in 1885, including scattered references of minimal significance. Cecilia Murphy (see below) also offers a full bibliography. Since these bibliographies are available, I here list, with comments, only the primary sources that I have found most useful. All that I can say even for these is that they supply a few details and enable us here and there to check Schallenberger's accuracy.

Thomas A. Baker's reminiscences. These are to be found in Thelma B. Miller, *History of Kern County, California* (2 vols.; Chicago, 1929), I, 122-127. Baker, as boy and young man, knew Stevens from 1863 until his death. He preserves some interesting anecdotes of the old man, but what he has to say about the journey of 1844 is of little importance, and much of it is not correct.

H. H. Bancroft, *Chronicles of the Builders of the Commonwealth* (7 vols.; San Francisco, 1891-1892). The section on the Murphys (Vol. III, chap. 2) is based chiefly on *Pen Pictures*, from which it quotes largely, but with no acknowledgment. A few details, however, are apparently from other sources, which may be the Murphy manuscripts (see below).

H. H. Bancroft, *History of California* (7 vols.; San Francisco, 1884-1890). References to Bancroft in the text are to this work unless otherwise indicated. The account of the Stevens Party (IV, 445-448, 454, n.) is valuable for its bibliography but is a secondary authority except for a few details.

Edmund Bray, "Memoir of a Trip to California, 1844." (MS in the Bancroft Library) Bray's memoirs are valuable, but very brief. Generally his dates are demonstrably inaccurate.

Call. An article in the San Francisco *Call*, September 13, 1864, is entitled "An Old Pioneer Company." It is not signed, but is stated to be by "A Lady of this City." Bancroft suggests "perhaps Mrs. Montgomery," and I would concur. The article is brief and of little importance.

H. S. Foote (ed.), *Pen Pictures from the Garden of the World* (Chicago, 1888). For Schallenberger's work in relation to this volume, see "The Text." *Pen Pictures* also offers biographies of several other members of the Stevens Party. Of particular interest is that of Schallenberger (pp. 56-57), which is based presumably on information supplied by him. "Story of the Murphy Party" was reprinted in the San Jose *Pioneer* (March 15, April 15, 1893), with only minor variations.

J. M. Guinn, *History of the State of California and Biographical Record of Coast Countries, California* (Chicago, 1904), pp. 494-496. (Editions vary; the Schallenberger material is omitted from some of them, and the pagination varies, without warning.) This biographical notice is of some value, particularly for the earlier and later life of Schallenberger. It is apparently based upon material furnished by Schallenberger, or some member of his family, independently of what he had previously written. By this time, he was nearly eighty, and 1844 was sixty years in the past. Nevertheless there are remarkably few inconsistencies with the earlier narrative and most of these are trivial. For instance, the number of coyotes hung up to freeze has risen from eleven to thirteen.

Sarah Winnemucca Hopkins, *Life among the Piutes* (Boston, 1883). This granddaughter of Truckee was a very small child in 1844, but her confused memories of the coming of the whites are not without interest.

Charles Kelly, *Old Greenwood* (Salt Lake City, 1936). Mr. Kelly, one of our foremost western trail-finders, is enthusiastically pro-Greenwood. As I have stated (see "The Leadership"), I cannot always agree with him. Kelly is a secondary authority on the Stevens Party except in so far as he preserves material from "Mr. W. J. Williams . . . whose mother was Lydia Patterson of the Murphy party of 1844." (I find no other mention of a Lydia Patterson, but this may well be the proper form of the name listed as "Tedra (?)" in Bancroft's "Pioneer Index.") Kelly does not state what part of his account is based on Williams's material, but it was apparently that on pp. 56-57 telling of the death of John Greenwood's wife and some encounters with Indians "beyond Ft. Laramie." At least, I know of no other source for these incidents. Curiously, Schallenberger is here cited as authority, although nothing of this sort is to be found in any Schallenberger document I have seen, and nothing of his except the San Jose *Pioneer* reprint is listed in

Kelly's Bibliography. Since dramatic incidents of this kind would scarcely have been omitted by other memorialists, I think that there must be some confusion.

Murphy manuscripts. Unsigned manuscripts dealing with the Murphy party in the Bancroft Library (especially, C-D 792) give a good deal of information about that family, and some details of the journey.

Cecilia Mary Murphy. "The Stevens-Murphy Overland Party of 1844." (M.A. thesis, University of California, typescript, 1941.) Miss Murphy (no relation to the Martin Murphy family) has compiled an excellent bibliography, and has pieced together the story in considerable detail from her sources, without subjecting them to much critical analysis.

Post. An unsigned account, apparently based on an interview, entitled "Captain Elisha Stevens," appeared in the San Francisco *Daily Evening Post,* December 26, 1883. This is important for information on Stevens but does not deal much with the journey.

Hugh Quigley, *The Irish Race in California* (San Francisco, 1878), pp. 177-183, 195-214. This is mainly a eulogy of the Murphy family and of James Miller, but gives some details of the trip not elsewhere available.

Moses Schallenberger's reminiscences. (See "The Text.") One of his letters is partially reproduced in C. F. McGlashan's *History of the Donner Party* (various editions), chap. v. It deals with the experiences at Donner Lake.

W. F. Swasey, *The Early Days and Men of California* (Oakland, 1891). Swasey gives a biography of Schallenberger (pp. 161-172) which is taken from *Pen Pictures.* Most of it consists of a highly inaccurate rendering of Schallenberger's own account, but no statement as to source is made. Although quotation marks are used, the text is freely altered. This book deserves to be cited chiefly as a warning that the use of quotation marks is no guarantee of accuracy.

www.ingramcontent.com/pod-product-compliance
Lightning Source LLC
Chambersburg PA
CBHW021714230426
43668CB00008B/827